Reclaiming the Christian Faith

Reclaiming the Christian Faith

Charles H. Bayer

ST. LOUIS, MISSOURI

Copyright © 2008 by Charles H. Bayer

All rights reserved. No part of this book may be reproduced or transmitted in any form or by any means, electronic or mechanical, including photocopying, recording, or by any information storage and retrieval system, without permission in writing from the copyright owner. For permission to reuse content, contact Charles Bayer at 694 Avery Road, Claremont, CA 91711.

Library of Congress Control Number: 2008929064
ISBN: 978-1-60350-001-2

Published by Lucas Park Books
www.lucasparkbooks.com

Contents

Introduction		1
1	The Rise of the Neocons	9
2	The Rise of the Christian Right	17
3	The Perfect Political Storm	25
4	Where the Evangelicals May Have It Right	35
5	Where the Evangelicals May Have It Wrong	41
6	Issues Vital to Evangelicals	51
7	The Distressing Retreat of The Liberal Church	59
8	Re-visioning the Progressive Church	69
9	The Public Face of Progressive Religion	75
10	Taking Back the Christian Faith—By One of Us at a Time	89
Addendum: A Progressive Manifesto for Christians in the United States		95
Conclusion		105

Introduction

"I no longer can refer to myself as a Christian. It is just too embarrassing. People assume that you are one of 'those' political right-wingers, who have not only seriously distorted the Christian faith, but have also taken it over." That statement is one of a number I have gotten, and is typical of what many solid colleagues are saying. If Christian means what the media describes it as representing, they don't want to be tarred with that brush.

When the press reports that "Christians" believe this or that, or that "Christians" form an important political bloc, we know whom they are talking about. And many of us refuse to be caught in that net. So we call ourselves "progressives" or take on some other protective coloring.

The fact is, a significant portion of the American conservative church has now been captured by the political right wing. Much of American Christianity has been seduced! Liberal Christians no longer are seen as authentic representatives of the ministry of Jesus, and the institutions which flow from that ministry. Herein lies one of the most significant religious facts of this young century.

It is time the Christian faith was reclaimed by a church clear about the solid implications flowing from the life and ministry of the one who came proclaiming that the commonwealth of God was at hand. Meanwhile, "progressive," formerly called "liberal," Christian institutions are in serious decline. While vital pockets, whose strength and commitment cannot be discounted, remain and even flourish, some former advocates of authentic faith have lost their nerve, their reason for being, a sense that their future will be any brighter than their dismal present. More than a handful of older "liberals" are convinced that the day of progressive denominations and their congregational units is now over. Significant numbers have abandoned what they consider moribund ecclesial structures. They no longer "do church." One correspondent suggests that Christianity may survive, but denominations and their inter-church structures may not. He is not alone in his judgment. Others hang onto their religious social groups, but hold little hope that these institutions have much of a future. According to another correspondent, "church" these days is like sitting beside the bed of a dying old friend, sharing stories of bygone days. Yet, pockets of progressive strength still provide enough hope that for many they are worth holding on to — and still can generate enough strength to challenge a distortion which identifies right-wing political causes with Christian faith.

While progressive Christian faith is in serious eclipse, Christian rhetoric and Christian institutions in other forms, however, have not disappeared from the public scene. They may currently be as powerful and as vital as they have been throughout American history. These alternate forms of Christianity seem to be alive and well.

Franz Kafka tells about the hunger artist, who would spend his summers in the town square, sitting in a straw-strewn cage and *not* eating. For years the townsfolk would gather at that site to watch his slow decline. It was the only show in town. However, over time interest in observing a man starving himself diminished. At his death...

> ...they buried the hunger artist along with the straw. But in his cage they put a young panther. Even for a person with the dullest mind it was clearly refreshing to see this wild animal throwing itself around in this cage, which had been dreary for such a long time. It lacked nothing. Without thinking about it for any length of time, the guards brought the animal food. It enjoyed the taste and never seemed to miss its freedom. This noble body, equipped with everything necessary, almost to the point of bursting, also appeared to carry freedom around with it. That seem to be located somewhere or other in its teeth, and its joy in living came with such strong passion

from its throat that it was not easy for spectators to keep watching. But they controlled themselves, kept pressing around the cage, and had no desire to move on.[1]

While liberal religious structures may currently be seen as slowly starving to death, the new panthers in the community may be Christian evangelicals. An informal survey of America's secularists asked the question, "How would you define today's Christians?" The overwhelming answers suggested that they were Bible believing, born-again, deeply conservative members of a variety of churches. The designations "fundamentalist" and "evangelical" were used interchangeably. Few respondents referred to Methodists, Presbyterians or any of the other former mainline, now sideline, denominations. When asked to identify today's most important Christian leaders, Pat Robertson, the late Jerry Falwell and James Dobson were the most common names mentioned. When asked who might be religious leaders in the liberal establishment, there were few answers.

Questions regarding Christian moral values inevitably produced two responses: homosexual marriage and abortion.[2] There is a religious fixation and fascination on these sexual issues—about which Jesus had nothing to say—while the issues of violence, injustice and marginalization, about which Jesus had a great deal to say, are avoided.

No single term for these emerging Christians and their churches seems adequate. Many "evangelicals" do not fall easily into the types and categories we will be using throughout this book. Many progressives also think of themselves as evangelicals. The term, "evangelical" came into currency several decades ago. Evangelicals were those who were primarily concerned about personal salvation. It was paired with its opposite, "ecumenical," denoting those who held a broader notion of Christian faith. "Liberal," the companion term of ecumenical, was often an appellation of derision, and in many quarters, still is. Now both terms, "evangelical" and "ecumenical" are used more broadly than their original designations.

Jim Wallis, of Sojourners, is among a significant number of believers who call themselves "evangelicals," even while they may also comfortably fit into the "progressive" camp.

The term "conservative" is used so loosely it has little meaning. "Fundamentalist" first referred to those who between 1910 and 1915 published a series of short books titled *A Testimony to the Truth*, which defined a series of Christian fundamentals. Among them were Biblical inerrancy, the virgin birth and substitutionary atonement through the blood of Christ. There are, however, significant pockets of fundamentalists who fall outside our discussion. They may be members of pietistic or simple-life sects, or just believers who hold deeply rooted notions flowing from Biblical inerrancy. In this book we will really be talking about those Christians who are members of conservative bodies, and who have made common cause with right-wing political operatives. They may be fundamentalists, evangelicals, members of progressive churches, or not part of any organized religious body. In fact, we will suggest that political forces have kidnapped significant portions of several branches of contemporary Christian faith and its institutions. So we will use the designation, "the religious right wing," or just "the religious right," to identify those we believe have been kidnappers of authentic faith—mostly with the complicity, if not the approval, of many other progressive church members.

When in these pages the term, "evangelical" occasionally appears, it is only an acknowledgment that this is the term the people to whom I am referring most often use for themselves. These Christians do not call themselves "right wingers," or "the Christian right." I learned long ago that when you describe some other group, particularly where you have a disagreement, it is appropriate to use the designation they use for themselves. Thus occasionally the term "evangelical" will appear, recognizing that the word covers far more ground than the Christian right.

While the rise of Christian fundamentalism both in the United States and in much of the rest of the world is well documented elsewhere, we will be particularly focused on how it has reshaped political life and the U.S.'s national political agenda, and at the same time been reshaped by them.

If this concern has critical political and societal implications, at root the problem is theological. The Christian right has seriously distorted, misrepresented, and compromised notions central to Jesus' concerns for the just society; what he from first to last referred to as the Reign or Commonwealth of God. The question is not whether liberal, formerly mainline, denominations and their agencies can recapture the Christian center from its political kidnappers, but whether Christian faith, apart from any ecclesial or denominational allegiance, can reemerge as a witness to Jesus' image of God's Commonwealth on earth as it is in heaven. If that can happen, what are the necessary steps along the way? In later sections of this book we will examine a possible scenario.

It is not the first time that religion has been successfully bought off by potent political forces. Throughout Christian history there has been a steady assault by political operatives, seeking to use the church, its people and its institutions, to accomplish what the politicians could not accomplish without it. In 1054 Pope Urban II was convinced by European mercantile interests that the prosperity of the Western world depended on opening up the trade routes to the East, then solidly in the hands of certain Muslim powers. Without the support of the Church, Europe was without the resources, the personnel or the ideological substructure to break open the way to Asia's riches. When Urban II declared it was the will of God that the sacred shrines of Christendom be freed from the infidels, the way was cleared to accomplish what merchants and politicians could not do alone. *"Deus Vult"* brought the Church into the effort, and ushered into history three centuries of tragedy, bloodshed and infidelity.

While most Christians historically have both understood and attempted to follow Jesus' notion of the just society, on numerous other occasions powerful political forces have subverted and seduced substantial aspects of Christian faith. Beyond the Crusades, consider the Inquisition, the Salem witch trials, slavery and segregation in the American South, apartheid in South Africa—just to name a few occasions where the church has been captured and used. This brief list only scratches the surface.

And what about this quote from another "Christian" culture:

"Hence today I believe that I am acting in accordance with the will of the Almighty Creator: by defending myself against the Jew, I am fighting for the work of the Lord."

Hitler was appointed Chancellor of the Weimar Republic January 30, 1933, and given dictatorial powers two months later. While he did not command a popular mandate, many believed that his power was the only hope for bringing a dispirited Germany out of the difficulties inherent in the Weimar catastrophe. The Third Reich promised a new sense of national security and purpose. Hitler needed the support of every aspect of German society, and this included the church.

About the time he became Chancellor, in an effort to consolidate his power, Hitler declared that in the new Germany there must be *"ein Volk* (one people), *ein Reich,* (one regime) *eine Glaube"* (one faith). He affirmed that the Christian faith would safeguard the soul of the German people. Thus began the German Christian movement. He continued:

> "The national government will consider as its supreme and first task that of restoring the spirit of unity and purpose among our people. It will preserve and defend the foundations upon which the power of our nation depends. It will take Christianity under its firm protection, as the basis of our entire morality."[3]

Much of the church, Protestant and Catholic, became so profoundly caught up in the passions of nationalism that Christian faith became identified with the economic, social, and political plans of the Third Reich. Enough of the Church was therefore so committed to this national ethos that Hitler was able to cobble together a working majority.

This kidnapping of religion in the service of a political agenda ought to provide a sufficient warning to contemporary America that it must realize the danger and resist a similar seduction.

A small minority of Christians fought to forestall this kidnapping. Under the leadership of Karl Barth and others, they met in Barmen on May 30, 1934 and drafted a resolution. At its heart is the affirmation that the Church belongs to Jesus Christ and is under his authority, and cannot be the handmaiden of any political regime.

> "We repudiate the false teaching that the church can and must recognize yet other happenings and powers, images and truths as divine revelation alongside this one Word of God...We repudiate the false teaching that there are areas of our life in which we belong not to Jesus Christ, but another lord...We repudiate the false teaching that the church can turn over the form of her message and ordinances at will or according to some dominant ideological and political convictions.[4]

Barth had previously held that "(the church) preaches (the gospel) *in* the Third Reich, but not *under* it, or in its spirit.[5]

Christianity is not the only world religion to be subject to kidnapping by powerful political interests. Consider the following two statements:

> "God has revealed to me that those doing battle for Allah and our country and meet death will immediately go to Heaven."[6] "God is on our side, and Satan is on the side of the United States."

The question therefore arises: Is there a sufficient impetus and will within the current American religious right to free itself from the political tyranny that is successfully using it for goals far removed from the integral focus of Christian faith? The question, and its far larger ramifications, has worldwide as well as national implications. I am convinced that buried within the evangelical movement there is both the will and the power to set itself free from this newly hatched political tyranny. I am also convinced that there is enough energy in modest pockets of the progressive Christian movement to accomplish the recovery of an authentic ecclesial presence, which can reinterpret the meaning of Christian faith for our times.

The fuller answer, however, may lie not in any current Christian structure, but in the God-given ability of people of faith to develop new forms of ecclesial witness. Portions of the religious right may rediscover the gospel. Portions of the progressive church may find again the world-changing power of Jesus' vision. New interchurch, interfaith and intercultural bodies may move into the void created by the kidnapped right-wing church and the moribund progressive church. Individuals may arise, not tied to any religious structure, but who embody a salvific vision of a new day. And then there is always that which is beyond any human planning or purposing. Never shortchange the amazing things that God, who is involved in every aspect of history and life, can accomplish without our approval or even our knowledge.

Notes

[1] Franz Kafka "The Hunger Artist." A short story, 1924 translated by Ian Johnson of Malespina College British Columbia 2004.

[2] The author talked to about 120 individuals, not of his acquaintance. These brief interviews took place on the street, in airplanes, and during a month spent in a Midwestern city before the 2004 election. The term "homosexual marriage" is generally used by those who oppose it, while the term "same-sex marriage" is the preferred term of its advocates.

[3] Quoted by James Dunn *The Justice of God* Paternoster Press London 1933 p.172.

[4] John H. Leith *Creeds of the Churches* Atlanta, John Knox Press 1982 pp. 520-521.

[5] Karl Barth *Zwischen und Zeiten* edition 11 1933 pp. 51-52.

[6] The Ayatollah Khomeini 1984.

CHAPTER 1

The Rise of the Neocons

The rise of right-wing religion in the United States parallels a similar political phenomenon in recent American history. To understand how the political right managed to co-opt and seduce the religious right requires an examination of the growth of each. Our story begins with how a new group of writers, thinkers, and operatives managed to take over the Republican Party. The details of this takeover are thoroughly documented in two carefully researched books, whose findings have gone unchallenged.[1] There follows only a brief summary of the critical events and the pivotal relevant documents.

In the 1980s, as the Cold War was winding down, a new political movement began to develop, originated within a handful of think tanks, which sprung out of well-funded solid conservative soil. It first of all confronted the traditional social and economic conservatives within the Republican Party, called the Realists. Nelson Rockefeller, Barry Goldwater and President George H. W. Bush had been prime examples of this Realist political understanding.

Strangely enough, early powerful members of this group came directly from the older, far-left political school. Irving Kristol, one of the early founders of the Neoconservative movement, held that these new Republicans tended to support a strong federal government, not a weak one. The Realists, on the other hand, had long insisted on limited government, individual freedom, a disavowal of nation building, and a foreign policy which was dedicated to keeping the United States out of struggles in other parts of the world.

The emerging group of political thinkers and strategists was convinced that America's future lay in a "unipolar" worldview. By that they meant a U.S. foreign policy, which saw this nation as the world's unrivaled power—militarily and economically. While world domination might be too strong an appellation, a critical reading of early documents produced by members of the group leaves little doubt that no challenge to American hegemony ought to be allowed. We will look at the centerpiece of these documents shortly.

One subset of the new political activists within the neocon family referred to themselves as the "Vulcans." The term had its genesis in the Roman god of fire and forge, and was borrowed from a statue of that name in Birmingham, Alabama. The Vulcans were to become central players in the Administration of President George W. Bush. You will recognize their names: Cheney, Rumsfeld, Wolfowitz and Rice.

Late in 2000, a Washington think tank, The Project for the New American Century, released a document that became the centerpiece of the foreign policy for these newly hatched "neocons."[2]

This document imaged a dramatic departure from prevailing American foreign policy, particularly espoused by the conservative Realists. It called for a military arsenal that would constitute the world's unrivaled power. Consider the following quotations from the report.

> There may be a need to develop a new family of nuclear weapons designed to address new sets of military requirements, such as would be required in targeting the very deep underground, hardened bunkers, that are being built by many of our potential adversaries.[3]

Thus the later advent of the "bunker busters."

> For one thing (our new policy of policing the world) will demand American leadership rather than that of the United Nations.[4]

> The UN is bypassed. U.S. policy will not only be unrivaled, it will be unilateral.

> (The control of space) is not an avoidable issue...For the U.S. armed forces to assert military preeminence, control of space...and an ability to deny others the use of space is an essential element in our military strategy.[5]

We will dominate everybody's space unilaterally!

Before the events of September 11, 2001, plans were already underway to take on Iraq in order to establish a substantial American presence in that part of the world. The report reads:

> The United States has for decades sought to play a more permanent role in Gulf regional security. While the unresolved conflict with Iraq provides the immediate justification, the need for a substantial American force presence in the Gulf transcends the regime of Saddam Hussein.[6]

Thus the reason for there being no exit strategy in our war against Iraq is that we had no intention of eventually leaving!

This document became the centerpiece of American foreign policy in the George W. Bush Administration. In September 2002, under the signature of the President, there was released, "The National Security Strategy of the United States of America." This official document mirrored the earlier report and was based on it, and its authors were, no doubt, many of those who had drafted the earlier statement. Beyond that, it takes the findings of the earlier statement and expands a number of its implications.

Consider this excerpt from the President's document.

> (We will destroy) the threat before it reaches our borders. While the United States will constantly strive to enlist the support of the international community, we will not hesitate to act alone, if necessary, to exercise our right of self-defense, by acting preemptively against such terrorists...[7]

Here lies the justification for our preemptive strike against Iraq. Even more appalling is the consistent policy of the Bush Administration in pursuing this policy on a worldwide basis.

The President's January 20, 2005 State of the Union address was a declaration that the aim of the United States was to promote and establish "liberty" in every nation in the world. The foes of "liberty" would have to yield to the hunger for freedom of any enslaved or otherwise oppressed people. The enemies of the "enslaved," who suffer in undemocratic regimes, would be our enemies. The central purpose of this Administration, said the President, was to promote democracy "in every nation and culture, with the ultimate goal of ending tyranny in our world." While couched in seemingly high-minded democratic words, it was in reality a velvet-covered brick. This is the same doctrine that determined we should go to war against Iraq. That doctrine was now to be extended throughout the globe. Even a cursory reading of the previously published position of the neocons would make it clear that their articulated doctrine had become America's foreign policy.

In an earlier State of the Union address, the President had already declared Iraq, Iran, and North Korea to be the Axis of Evil. Iraq seemed to be only the first of this trilogy to be invaded, with devastating results. As a result of our occupation, estimates ranging from 150,000 to 600,000 Iraqis have been destroyed, many of them children. In the process, 4,000 American soldiers have been killed and tens of thousands maimed. Simultaneously, the reputation of the United States around the world was shredded.

In pursuit of the imperialistic doctrine promulgated by the neocons and supported by the President, nations beyond the three previously named have been added to the group of potential adversaries. In her confirmation hearings as Secretary of State, Condoleezza Rice expanded the list to include Cuba, Burma, Belarus, and Zimbabwe. Other Administration officials have added Russia, Pakistan, China, Syria, and Egypt as "illustrations" of those who would feel the impact of this newly devised U.S. foreign policy.

The radical unipolar doctrine first propounded by the Project for the New American Century had clearly become the operating principle of the Bush Administration. In March 2005 the President nominated John R. Bolton as the United States Ambassador to the United Nations. Bolton, a self-proclaimed bomb-thrower, was a long-time unipolarist. On February 3, 1994 in a "Global Structures Convocation," he is reported to have said:

> There is no such thing as the United Nations. ...There is an international community that occasionally can be led by the only real power left in the world and that is the United States, when it suits our interest and we can get others to go along. And I think it would be a real mistake to count on the U.N. as if it is some disembodied entity out there that can function on its own.[8]

Bolton in another venue went on to indicate that there should be just one permanent member of the Security Council, and that is the United States.

The question arises; how was this radical set of policies sold to the American people? What coalition of forces first managed to take over the Republican Party and finally elect a President whose Administration based its foreign policy on such an outlandish and fundamentally un-American set of policies? It is my thesis that this alteration in the basic perspective of the United States would not have been accomplished without the support of an American religious movement centered in the evangelical right-wing constituency, which was successfully seduced.

One may doubt, however, that when the religious right signed on as supporters of a prayerful, devout, born-again Christian President, they realized what would come with that package. How at this juncture, can the millions of well-intentioned, thoughtful Christians, who have been thus seduced, rediscover the heart of the Christian gospel and retrace their steps? What needs to happen to help these people of general good will realize that the political doctrine of the neocons, and thus of the Bush Administration, is a far cry from the teachings, the intent, and the will of Jesus of Nazareth?

Tied to this new unipolar foreign policy are significant implications for a revised domestic agenda. For many years, prior to coming to power of the neocons, conservative politicians have bristled at the New Deal and its implications for a more egalitarian society. From FDR on, substantial Democratic majorities have not only supported New Deal policies, but also managed to significantly expand the social safety net.

How does the neocon's radical international policy manage to seriously reduce this enormously popular long-term vision of a more just society? Consider how the shredding of the social safety net has already begun to happen. The cost of the Iraq war, including the enormous funding granted to the military establishment, has generated a multi-trillion dollar Federal deficit. This in the face of the significant surpluses developed in the last Administration. The problem has been exacerbated by large tax reductions substantially going to our more affluent citizens.

In the name of fiscal responsibility, the Administration vowed to draw down the deficit. The only way this can be made possible is by the reduction of programs which support a more egalitarian society—that is the social safety net. In the President's 2005 proposed budget, scores of these programs were eliminated or seriously reduced. In addition, the appointment of conservative judges to the Federal bench, beginning with the Supreme Court, significantly continues to change the political dynamics.

President Bush had long supported a society that rewards the rich and punishes the poor. It is reported that during his MBA program at Yale, he remarked to one of his professors that the poor were poor because they were lazy and indolent.

An opening salvo in the attack on New Deal policies came early in 2005 when the President suggested the partial privatization of Social Security. Already Medicare and other health-related efforts had come under serious attack. The President's "ownership society" seemed right for those who already own most everything, and wrong for those struggling from paycheck to paycheck, let alone America's most fragile.

Can these sets of policies really represent values, which flow from the Christian gospel? If not, then how is it that so many faithful Christians managed to buy them when they took on the support of a devout President? That is the question every faithful Christian must answer. My guess is that significant numbers of them will begin to see the larger implications, which they have inherited through their seduction.

Notes

[1] *The Rise of the Neocons* by James Mann Viking Press New York 2004.
Imperial Designs by Gary Dorrien, Routledge New York 2004.
These two books trace in great details the advent of this conservative political movement within the Republican Party. I have only sketched out a few of the broad strokes of what is a much more detailed phenomenon.

[2] *Rebuilding America's Defenses—strategy , forces and resources for a new century* Project for the New American Century, Washington, DC.2000 Among the familiar names attached to the report were William Kristol, Frank Gaffney, Donald Kagan, Charles Krauthammer, Richard Perle, Norman Podhoretz, Paul Wolfowitz, H. Lewis Libby. These and other contributors to the document hold important places in the George W. Bush Administration.

[3] Ibid p. 8.
[4] Ibid p.11.
[5] Ibid p. 55.
[6] Ibid p. 14.
[7] *The National Security Strategy of the United States,* The White House, Washington , D.C. 2002.
[8] Reported in the Los Angeles Times March 9, 2005.

CHAPTER 2

The Rise of the Christian Right

The story of the Christian right, and its relationship to political power, did not originate just in the last two decades. From the beginning of the American enterprise, there has been a steady record of political power based on a religious commitment. The story of the conquest of what is now Central and South America, basically by Christians from the Iberian Peninsula, is a critical part of our hemispheric history.

In the Colonies—to eventually become the United States—conservative religion played a significant political role. The fundamentalist Puritans, to be distinguished from the more liberal Pilgrims of the Plymouth Colony, attempted to establish what was essentially a theocracy in places like Salem, Massachusetts.

In the second decade of the 19th century John Nelson Darby, ideological leader of the English Plymouth Brethren, developed a dispensational theology that on this side of the Atlantic became the basis of new forms of sectarianism. The Plymouth Brethren found an American colleague in Dwight L. Moody of Chicago. The explicit second coming of Christ and the premillenialism that accompanied it slowly evolved into the basis of what was later to be called fundamentalism.

As slavery took hold in the Colonies, there developed a need to defend the practice on religious grounds. In the American South, the political power, long centered in a one-party system, supported the institution. Both in the antebellum and in the later segregationist South, the Party—to become the Democratic Party, and the quasi-established Protestant, Church could not be distinguished from each other. They were composed of the same males. While African Americans, slave or free, were not entitled to vote, neither were women. Indeed, most Southern men turned over the public reins to a conservative religious oligarchy. Closer to the center than to the fringes of society were the Ku Klux Klan and later the White Citizens' Councils. If the Klan met in fields on Saturday nights to burn crosses, they met on Sunday mornings in Baptist and Methodist churches to worship them.

Forty percent of the Baptist clergy were actually slave owners. Those clerics who held no human property were probably too poor to do so. In the mainline congregation I once served in Missouri, a former minister had offered a reward to any parishioner who would cross the river into Kansas and recapture his two runaway slaves. The year was 1860. On one occasion I was the guest preacher in an Oklahoma congregation. The front cover of the pulpit Bible had stamped in gold the words, "Presented by the Ku Klux Klan."

Church-going is what practically everyone respectable Southern gentleman did on Sunday. Few societies have been more thoroughly controlled by a "Christian" mentality. It should also be noted that the Southern church, with few exceptions, was a hard-core fundamentalist enterprise. Slavery, and then segregation, were stoutly defended on the basis of Biblical truth. One might wonder if church growth and the saturation of the population with religion are really an evidence that the "commonwealth of God has come near." Historically Christians have always been able to find scriptural passages that defended policies of exclusion and bigotry.[1] The more thoroughly the society was made up of people with a common religion, the more likely that society would tend to be exclusivist, unwelcoming, and xenophobic.

The revivals, known as the Great Awakenings, while concerned with individual wholeness and employing a clear evangelical perspective, were simultaneously rooted in issues of justice. This is particularly true in relationship to the abolition of slavery. The Northern churches, however, tended to be far more open and liberal than the churches of the South. Thus the Civil War produced a split in Methodist, Presbyterian, and Baptist denominations. Other bodies divided over economic or sociological issues. While there are notable exceptions, the more conservative the church the more it was inclined to side with conservative political ideologies and parties. The obverse was generally true among the more liberal churches.

Beyond the issues of slavery and segregation, conservative churches tended to eschew politics. Slavery was seen as a moral or values matter, not as particularly political. The rejection of evolution and the prohibition of alcoholic beverages were also matters of religious, not partisan political, concerns.

Beyond the United States and beyond the Christian religion, whenever fundamentalism consumes any significant body of the faithful, it tends to incorporate an exclusivist and militant response to those not part of the religious group. It is equally as intolerant of those of the faith considered to be unorthodox. Jewish, Islamic, and Hindu fundamentalists can be counted on to support and be supported by the right-wing political systems wherever the religion is found to be in a substantial majority.[2]

The term "fundamentalism" can be traced back to 1910-1915 and the publication of a series of paperback books defending the "fundamentals" of the faith. The intellectual center of the movement was generated by a coterie of scholars at Princeton University. The internal academic debate, however, produced a split. The minority was led by J. Gresham Machen, who eventually left Princeton to found his own academic institution, Westminster Theological Seminary. However, even Machen was too liberal for Carl McIntire, who split from him to found the Philadelphia College of the Bible.

McIntire spent his life fighting the liberal church. He would appear at almost every significant ecumenical or denominational gathering spewing his own form of vindictiveness against the modernists he believed had seriously distorted Christian truth. McIntire complained that these liberals were more concerned about their social agenda then they were about salvation in Jesus and the accompanying Biblical authenticity. While he stayed clear of American politics, for years he was a stout defendant of Ian Pasley of Northern Ireland, and supported

Pasley's continual struggle against Catholicism. Pasley became a Member of Parliament, where he managed to perpetuate his fight against the "Papists" only mellowing in the early years of the 21st Century when he saw the wisdom of a more conciliatory position.

Following World War II and the emergence of the Cold War, other right-wing religious figures draped themselves in the American flag and majored in the accusation that all non-fundamentalists were dupes of the Communist conspiracy—if not Communist themselves. Among them was Billy James Hargis, and his "Christian Anti-Communist Crusade." While McIntire and Hargis commanded the loyalty of significant numbers of middle-American religionists, no one with political power paid much attention to them. And indeed these firebrands made little effort to transform their followers into an effective political bloc.

The nomination of John F. Kennedy provided a political rallying point for significant numbers of evangelicals, who were deeply concerned about Kennedy's Catholicism and feared that were he elected, American policy would hereafter be made in the Vatican. Candidate Kennedy de-fanged the issue when at a large evangelical meeting he openly declared that he, as President, would not be under the control of the Pope. During his Presidency there was also concern among evangelicals over Kennedy's support of the Equal Rights Amendment to the Constitution, which they felt would compromise what they believed to be the biblically ordained dominant role of males.

When Richard Nixon became President, he sought the attention and support of Billy Graham, who became an ardent pro-Nixon apologist. Later in life Graham commented that this relationship was the one he most regretted. Nevertheless, this was an early indication that conservative Christians were beginning to pay attention to the possibility of political power, and yearned for some recognition from the White House. Nixon may also have been the first President to realize the potential political clout of conservative Christians. He adopted what became known as a Southern Strategy, which over time lured the formerly Democratic-solid South, which was also solidly evangelical, into the Republican camp.

The Rise of the Christian Right 21

Jimmy Carter, while a classic Democratic Liberal, was an effective, born-again Christian, who during his Presidential years regularly taught a Sunday School class in a Washington Baptist Congregation. This identification quickly drew evangelicals to him. Bailey Smith, then head of the Southern Baptist Convention, during the campaign suggested that the next President happily shared the same initials as the founder of the Christian faith—J.C. After his election, it quickly became apparent that Carter, while one of them, did not share the fundamentalists' political philosophy, and support of the Carter Administration by conservative Christians declined. A particular hesitancy on the part of the conservative church developed in the wake of Carter's advocacy of the Supreme Court decision in Roe v. Wade. Nevertheless Carter's native Southern religiosity stalled the march to the right of his fellow evangelicals.

Ronald Reagan, who was never more than nominally religious, saw the potential political influence of conservative religion and overtly wooed numbers of evangelical leaders. During his campaign for the Presidency, he appeared before a large evangelical assembly where he stated that although they could not endorse him, he endorsed them. Now evangelical leaders were welcome at the White House, and the relationship between Reagan's conservative political philosophy and the evangelical right began to take firmer shape.

The scene matured dramatically with the coming to public attention of two powerful religious leaders who saw religious conservatism and right-wing politics as sharing the same values and goals—Jerry Falwell and Pat Robertson.

In 1979 Paul Weyrich commented to Jerry Falwell, an independent Baptist minister in Lynchburg, Virginia, that he believed there was a moral majority out there ready to be organized. Falwell picked up the phrase and used it as the motto of a new organization. From the beginning the Moral Majority was not overtly a political organization, but with a change of name to the Christian Coalition, soon became transformed into one.

Falwell announced that Christian pastors had three ministerial goals: Get individuals to Jesus Christ. Get them baptized. Get them registered to vote. He realized that there was a vast reservoir of political power out there among unregistered Christian conservatives. One evangelical leader commented that conservative religious individuals constituted "the largest tract of virgin political power on the landscape."

As late as the 1980s only half of potential evangelical voters were registered, even in areas where otherwise the voter registration figures were much higher. Falwell was convinced that the time had arrived for conservative Christians to exert their political muscle, and openly disavowed any hesitancy to engage in electoral issues.

Already conservative constituencies had taken active roles in changing the shape of hundreds of local political jurisdictions, principally in the elections of local Library Boards, City Councils and School Boards. Yet many conservatives held that local politics was not politics at all, allowing them to do what conservatives up to this point had claimed never to do.

It also became apparent that these new aggressive conservative Christians had seen State Republican organizations as fair game, and by the mid-eighties had taken over eleven. Having gradually given up their aversion to politics, the scene was set for someone to come along who would enter the national political game on behalf of conservative Christians. That individual emerged in the person of Pat Robertson.

Robertson, an ordained minister and a graduate of Yale Law School, was the son of a former United States Senator from Virginia who had been a serious segregationist. Pat's commitment to conservative political causes was evidenced in his unsuccessful run for the Presidency in 1988. While he evidenced considerable strength in the early primaries, he was eventually defeated for the Republican nomination by George H. W. Bush. Even so, he was convinced that his earlier support of right-wing causes secured the Presidency for Ronald Reagan. Robertson was not greatly enamored with George H. W. Bush, who eventually was elected, and for much of the Bush Administration the thrust of conservative Christianity into places of political power was thwarted.

Robertson, however, was increasingly committed to the takeover of American politics by the Christian right. At the founding of the Christian Coalition, he said, "The mission of the

Christian Coalition is simple. It is to mobilize Christians—one precinct at a time, one community at a time—until once again we are the head and not the tail, and at the top rather than the bottom of our political system. We have enough votes to run this country, and when the people say, 'We've had enough,' we're going to take over."

Speaking to the American Center for Law and Justice in a 1993 address, he said, "There is no such thing as separation of church and state in the Constitution. It is a lie of the Left and we are not going to take it any more."

The Denver Post reported that Robertson said in 1992, "We want as soon as possible to see a majority of the Republican Party in the hands of pro-family Christians."

Robertson's popular and well-financed 700 Club provided a powerful outlet for these views. In later years he was nobly assisted by Fox News and a spate of right-wing radio talk shows, as well as a collection of television religionists who flooded the public airwaves with political propaganda under a quasi-Christian cover—and became amazingly wealthy in the process.

Armed with a powerful ideology, the popular issues of abortion, homosexual marriage and prayer in the public schools, the Christian Coalition was ready for a larger political assault. All they needed was a national political leader who could inspire this massive evangelical constituency to register and vote. And that person was just over the horizon.

Notes

[1] See my *A Resurrected Church*, Chalice Press St. Louis 2001 p 50 and following

[2] See for details and analysis *The Glory and the Power*, Martin E. Marty and R. Scott Appleby Beacon Press Boston 1992 These authors were the principals in The Fundamentalist Project, which spent a number of years analyzing the fundamentalist phenomenon in the United States and elsewhere in other nations and among other religious groups.

CHAPTER 3

The Perfect Political Storm

My wife and I ought to be listed in the Guinness Book of Records. We were the only passengers on a container ship traveling from Australia to Oakland California, when somewhere in the North Pacific we encountered an enormous storm. The waves were 60 feet high. Wendy broke her toe as we were thrown about our cabin. This German vessel had on board only two English language videos. At the height of the full gale, as we clutched a table anchored to the floor, we watched one of them. We are probably the only people to have viewed "The Perfect Storm" in the midst of one!

The movie, and book from which it is taken, describes three separate storm systems that met off the New England coast to form a single gigantic tempest.

Three intense political forces developed over the United States beginning in about 1990. Each has intensified in the years since. Together they have formed one mammoth political storm. They are:

- The takeover of the Republican Party by the neocons.
- The dramatic growth in size and intensity of a new politically engaged right wing among conservative Christians.
- The personal religious commitment of George W. Bush.

The perfect political storm, which developed when these three separate forces found each other, has changed the shape and direction of the United States, and with that change, the course of world history. So far we have looked briefly at the first two of these tempests. We turn now to the third partner in this potent trilogy; the coming to power of George W. Bush.

George W. Bush—the third storm

We must assume that the Christian piety of President Bush was honestly come by. We have no reason not to accept his story, and the story others tell of him. He was a young playboy. If not an alcoholic, he was at least a heavy drinker both in his college days and after. At one point he received a ticket for drunk driving near the Bush family compound in Kennebunkport, Maine. He was a mediocre Yale student, more inclined to hit the bottle than to hit the books.

Back in Texas following College, he dabbled unsuccessfully with a failing oil company and shared part ownership in a baseball team. He did poorly at both, even though by having the right friends he came away from his involvement with the Texas Rangers with a considerable profit.

Somewhere along the line he encountered a traveling evangelist who was walking through the world carrying a heavy wooden cross. Subsequently he was put in touch with Billy Graham, probably through a few friends who were concerned about his disastrous direction. His testimony is that he accepted Jesus as Lord and Savior, and swore off drinking forever. As with many other sincere people, this conversion experience changed his life. The genuineness of the encounter must be taken at face value. By all accounts, his conversion was not simply a political maneuver. He became a different, better, born-again man. And for that he deserves respect.

However, as he became a person of power, perhaps the most powerful person in the world, Bush fell into a trap that finally captures many people who are simultaneously very powerful and very religious. He assumed that God's will had become his by direct divine intervention. Because he was now righteous, what he did must be what God wanted him to do. God would not lead a faithful leader down the wrong path. God would direct his ways. If, indeed, he asked God what he should do—which he did—God would tell him. At one point Bush suggested that it was not his earthly father, George H. W.

Bush, but his "heavenly father" whose counsel and wisdom was his political guide.

While it would be ingenuous to suggest that Bush used his religious commitments for political advantage, there was a convenient match.

Three major players, therefore, found their fortunes about to coalesce, thus creating this enormous political storm. Consider again the trilogy and their major goals.

The neocons were advocates of a unipolar international perspective that was far out of the mainstream of American thought. Their first battle was with the traditional Republicans, the Realists who had controlled the Party for a generation. Because they were more thoughtful and possibly cleverer than the Realists, the neocons were able to take over much of the Party. The Realists in the Party, while not isolationists, did not believe in nation building, and were determined to keep the United States from playing the role of the world's policeman. The Realists also were committed to limited Federal government, balanced budgets and protective trade policies.

The neocons believed that it was the destiny of the United States to assume a worldwide power and authority so strong that no one could challenge our military or economic hegemony. Having wrested control of the Party from the Realists, the neocons still had a problem. They lacked a popular constituency large enough to win elections. They needed a more friendly Congress, and that implied an electorate, which supported their unipolar agenda. The American people, by and large, were in no mind to adopt this new world role. While the neocons were ideologically clear, their goals well articulated and their project enormous, as yet they did not have the support of the majority of Americans. They therefore looked for a large body of committed voters, which in turn would exert pressure on a reluctant Congress.

The religious right wing had an agenda far removed from that of the neocons. It was clearly focused in a set of political goals consisting of three overarching issues:

1-Abortion. 2-Homosexuality—particularly homosexual marriage. 3-Prayer in the public schools. The first two were matters of personal sexual morality. The third included the notion that the United States was, from the beginning, not only a Christian nation, but also embodied a specific moral code, which flowed from this religious base. As was the case with the neocons, while their ideology was clear, they did not have a sufficient active national constituency dedicated enough to control public policy either at the Executive or at the Legislative level. Clearly the Judiciary was generally opposed to their position on possibly every issue and at every level. Their main lack, however, was not having a charismatic religious figure at the highest level of government, who could command their political loyalty.

What is more, significant numbers of evangelicals were still suspicious of politics and did not believe that these issues could be dealt with at an electoral level. Thus through the year 2000, millions of those who were their potential supporters did not vote and were not even registered. Not since the Reagan Administration, had any President paid much attention to them, or agreed with their stand on the issues. Even so, their potential numbers were so large that if added to a traditional conservative constituency, they could form an electoral majority.

The neocons, aware of the dilemma, but controlling much of the Republican Party, determined to find a winning strategy and a Presidential candidate to go with it. The evangelicals, while certain of their rightness on the issues, had no leader with national stature who could succeed in mobilizing their potential swarm of voters. These two storms spun furiously just off the coast of the United States.

Into this vortex came a third force in the person of **George W. Bush**. It is uncertain whether the neocons saw his potential candidacy as the way to recruit the evangelicals, or the opportunity simply fell into their laps. What is certain is that he became their candidate. But before he could be politically useful to the neocons he had to be reeducated. His election in 2000 was by less than a shoestring. Some felt that the election was stolen, first by the manipulation of the vote in Florida, and subsequently by the 5 to 4 decision of the conservative majority on the Supreme Court. What is more, he came to power without a specific agenda. Not having a clear direction, his Administration sputtered during its first months.

The reprogramming of President Bush

Bush had campaigned and "won" the election on the basis that he was a uniter, not a divider, that he believed in a compassionate conservatism, that he eschewed nation building as an acceptable policy, and that his economic conservatism would maintain a balanced national budget and a greatly limited Federal establishment. How then was he to be persuaded to alter his course 180 degrees, and sign on to the agenda of the powerful neocons?

Two separate matters accomplished the job. First, Bush had been convinced that his closest advisors—the inner circle of his Administration—should be made up of the new rulers of the Republican Party. Remember the Vulcans? Cheney had already anointed himself as the Vice Presidential candidate. Bush had asked him to secure for the ticket the most appropriate person. Cheney selected himself from the list of possible office holders. With Cheney came Powell, Rumsfeld, Rice, Wolfowitz, Kristol, Armitage, Perle, and others. The inner circle of the already committed was now formed. They would become the driving intellectual force of the new Administration.[1]

The second factor turning Bush around was the tragic event which took place on September 11, 2001. "Terrorist" became the most important word in Bush's vocabulary. This event dramatically altered his course as well as having a profound influence on the entire nation.

With steady-handed coaching at the hands of the political right wing, the President became not only a neocon, but the chief neocon. The three storms had now merged. The new Republican unipolar internationalists had their leader, and the evangelical right-wing Christians had their spiritual hero—in the White House!

The seduction is accomplished

The seduction of conservative Christians was almost complete. The President not only agreed with them on their overarching issues, he seemed willing to put their agendas on his—big time! Millions of sincere Christians from evangelical and fundamentalist constituencies now gave themselves to the one person they trusted above all others, George W. Bush. More than any other occupant of the White House, Bush projected the sincere Christian piety that won the loyalty of millions of the born again, who formerly were skeptical of political involvement.

They were convinced he would not only talk their talk, but would also walk their walk. There would be a reversal of Roe v. Wade, courtesy of an altered make-up of America's Courts, beginning with the Supreme Court. Marriage and the family would be protected, particularly against the onslaught of the increasingly vocal homosexual community. There would be a Constitutional Amendment defining and defending marriage as a contract between one man and one woman. America would once again recognize its Christian heritage. Prayer would come back to civic life. Money would flow to Christian bodies in support of socially important work.

Bush also saw the world beyond these key issues much as they saw them. Almost all world affairs could be reduced to a battle between good and evil. We were the good. Evil was incarnate in our enemies, the terrorists, and ultimately in Saddam Hussein.

History was leading to the final victory of God over the citadels of evil. It would finally be fulfilled in the rapture of the righteous. Conservative Christians had a spate of popular books including twelve "Left Behind" novels—spelling it all out. A generation back, an early right-wing Christian, James Watt, the Secretary of the Interior, had told a Congressional Committee that protecting natural resources was unimportant in the light of the imminent return of Jesus Christ. He said in his public testimony, "After the last tree is felled, Christ will come back." A 2004 Gallup Poll suggested that fully one third of the American populace believed in the theory of the rapture. And these true believers were registering to vote in massive numbers.

While Bush never seemed to overtly mention the rapture, he did talk consistently about good vs. evil. Here was a man of faith and prayer, who had been saved by the power and love of Christ, and they would follow him!

Having celebrated the validity of the President's leadership on matters that were important to them, many evangelicals lost all perspective about agendas and policies that had nothing to do with their religious commitments. But trusting the President in matters that they believed vital left them no choice but to trust him all the way. And that meant accepting the neocons' larger agenda. They bought the whole package, because there was no way they could buy only part of it. Thus, their seduction was secure, their political commitments recognized at the highest levels of government, and their values agenda finally affirmed.

The three separate storms had become one enormous tempest. And those in all three camps had come out winners. The neocons now had in their pocket a powerful constituency to be added to an already lively Republican base. With the right wing Christians in tow, winning elections was within easier reach.

George W. Bush had found, in the perspectives of the neocons, a set of issues that could save a faltering Presidency—a way to insure his political immortality.

In the package!

The religious right could at long last arrive at the center of political power, which could guarantee a successful resolution of all their important issues. But it was unaware that it had been seduced—sold a package in which they identified issues important to them. But buried in that same package was preemptive war, injustice, world domination, the total control of space, the sole right to have and use weapons of mass destruction, the torture of enemies, the loss of civil liberties, tax breaks for the wealthy, the ripping to shreds of the social safety net, the degradation of God's nature for the sake of profits, the hostility of much of the world's people, trillions of dollars of debt future generations will be forced to pay, the proliferation of weapons in the hands of practically everybody, the death penalty and a sordid collection of other things no thoughtful Christian could possibly countenance. How is it that so many solid religious people have bought this disastrous and un-Christian package? I can only conclude that they have been seduced. What they bought is not what they assumed came with an anti-same sex marriage and an anti-abortion agenda—issues about which Jesus had nothing to say.

Probably the one person who had the insight to put it all together was Carl Rove. With a clearer vision of the politically possible than anyone else on the scene, he saw the enormous potential in the conservative religious movement, and developed ways both to get it registered and then to deliver these newly registered enthusiasts to the polls. Rove did not need to be ideologically committed to their agenda. He was basically a political pragmatist with his eye only on what worked. He was a political craftsman whose job was to develop a plan leading to electoral victory. At that task he was extremely proficient.

Everybody wins

The neocons were content to sit back and let this happen. They had their President and they had their electoral majority. Many of the important thinkers in the neocon movement were not right-leaning Christians, or Christians at all, and had no particular brief for much the evangelicals championed. Wolfowitz, Perle, Podhoretz, Krauthammer, Wattheberg, Muravchik, the Kristols—father and son—Kagan, Boot and Kaplin were substantial to the brain trust that developed the neocon agenda.[2] And they knew where they were headed.

At this point it appeared almost impossible that the Christian right wing might realize it had been seduced, and thus escape its seducer. It seemed too deeply committed to the President, too certain that he would finally bring to fruition victory in the issues they cared about, and too oblivious of the central implications of the Christian faith they claimed to love. As of the election of 2004, their seduction seems complete. And yet, knowing many sincere evangelicals, I am convinced that they are at heart committed to what Jesus was committed to, and thus may be led to rethink the web of deceit that has trapped them.

Since the 2004 election the religious right has left no stone unturned in solidifying its political power. Huge rallies of conservative Christians, beginning with the clergy, have been held across America's heartland. Having nailed down an impressive political victory, evangelicals were unwilling to left lit drift away. Since George W. Bush was not eligible for reelection, other potential political stars were being groomed in the persons of Senators Frist, Brownback, and Santorum.

But Frisk retired, Santorum was defeated in his 2006 reelection bid, and Brownback remained a minor figure in the Republican hierarchy.

Beyond this trilogy of effective conservative Christian leaders, and through them, efforts were intensified to rearrange the nature of the American judiciary, first in the Federal Appeals Courts and finally in the Supreme Court of the United States. The appointment of two conservative Justices was a major step in reversing not only Roe v. Wade, but other progressive policies stretching back to the New Deal, including more recent civil rights advances.

For a while it appeared that the neocons had successfully captured all three branches of government, with the Administration now in total control of national policy. The fly—or was it an eagle—in the ointment was the increasingly unpopular war against Iraq. The 2006 Congressional elections interrupted the total consolidation of government by the neocons. At the same time, while George W. Bush retained enormous power, his increased unpopularity spelled the collapse of the cabal. The looming 2008 elections would determine the future of the American dream.

Yet even with the passing of George W. Bush from the scene, the relationship between conservative politics and conservative Christianity was too well fixed to collapse. While American politics seemed committed to move away from the agenda of the neocons, other forces needed to get to work if the Christian faith was to be reclaimed.

The year 2007 saw the beginning of what might be the breakup of evangelical solidarity. Many evangelicals became increasingly concerned about global warming and the larger ecological crisis. Others began to look with increased suspicion at the war against Iraq. If evangelicals were solid supporters of George W. Bush, no one candidate in the 2008 primary season captured their commitment.

Notes

[1] Gary Dorrien has produced a carefully constructed systematic analysis of the development of political power by the neocons. See his *Imperial Designs* Routledge New York 2004.
[2] Ibid Gary Dorrien.

CHAPTER 4

Where the Evangelicals May Have It Right

It has become easy for progressive Christians to write off their evangelical sisters and brothers. Angry at the ease with which solid conservative Christians have been seduced, many liberals are too quick to judge those whose take on the nature of the Christian faith differs from theirs. Perhaps there are significant areas of agreement we have not sufficiently explored. Beyond that, I believe there are serious lessons progressives need to learn from their more conservative colleagues. In this chapter we will examine just a few of the things evangelicals may have right—or at least partly right.

The abiding value of family life

Deeply embedded in the conservative heart is the importance of the family. Much of what appears to be hostile perspectives on issues such as abortion and same-sex marriage, comes from a fear that the family is under attack. By family they tend to mean the traditional nuclear family. It is difficult for many evangelicals to see family in any other constellation than mother, father, and the kids, all living happily together under the same roof. There are parts of the country, particularly in the rural heartland, where this notion of family was and is the economic base of community life. The sustainability of the farm depended on the integrity of the family unit. For many families the workday was not eight hours, but both mother and father labored from dawn to dusk. The children were put to work as soon as they were old enough to take directions. The family could not survive without their effort.

Family also tended to imply a certain hierarchy. The protector of the family, and thus the head, was the dominant male, or the father. He was often the only educated or well-read member of the family. There tended to be large numbers of children, and the mother's full-time job was their sustenance and nurture. Households where both mother and father worked outside the home were rare until the defense requirements of World War II. Democracy had little place in that sort of family. The father had to be the leader. Even if that age is slowly passing away, there are still the stories families tell about it, and retold stories often determine present attitudes.

The Apostle Paul is commonly cited, by evangelicals, as the authority for this hierarchical system. He speaks of the family as first the husband, then the wife, then the children, and at bottom of the pyramid, the servants or slaves. That is the way the well-ordered Greek family was structured, and Paul was simply recapitulating how things were in his world.[1]

Many evangelicals remain unaware that even in their churches, it is likely that the majority of people will live in constellations other than the nuclear family—single people of both genders, widows and widowers, persons of the same gender where sex is not an issue, people of the same gender where sex is part of their relationship, group homes, student dormitories, institutions—just to name a few. While family systems are undergoing enormous change, the fear is that the family is simultaneously suffering a steady decline in importance and sanctity. Evangelicals tend to see these changes as a degeneration of the traditional societal structure. While progressives seem better able to understand the validity of the various types of family structures, nevertheless the value of the family, in whatever form, cannot be discounted. Evangelicals may give more thought to the necessary solidity of the family than do many progressives. The argument that same-sex marriage just means more stable families and fewer non-legal partnership falls on deaf ears.

A recognition of the coarsening of culture

Evangelicals are also quicker to sense the general coarsening of the culture. High School teachers tell us that too much of their time must be spent in simply trying to keep order instead of productive classroom interaction and learning. While the sexual revolution has been liberating, it has also brought changes in language, and the proliferation of sexual activity reaching down to children. When few high school girls anymore will even admit to being virgins, evangelicals sense that there has been a cheapening of the sacredness of sex. The coarsening of both language and images, which come into every home with a television, causes concern for the stability of the culture. Many evangelicals feel that the loss of a religious base for culture, and its increased anti-religious atmosphere, is responsible for this degradation. Evangelicals seem quicker to point out that with privilege and opportunity there also comes responsibility.

An insistence on the question of values

Both the insecurity of the nuclear family and the coarsening of culture may be subsumed under a larger category, which is usually stated as, "values." At this point, progressives have had to hurry to catch up with evangelicals, even as we attempt to redefine and reinterpret the values issue. While progressives continue to talk about issues, evangelicals tend to talk about values, and with them values consistently trump issues.

The overriding importance of the church

Many evangelicals tend to take their relationship to the church far more seriously than do many progressives. Being members of the church is something they *are*, while for many progressives church is something they *do*—among a myriad of other activities, associations and organizations. There exists a serious ecclesial discipline among many conservatives. They not only talk about the value of small groups; most mega-churches are organized on the basis of these more intimate units.

The central importance of the Bible

Evangelicals tend to take the Bible and its study much more seriously than do many progressives. While the way they see the Bible may be fraught with superstition and a massive misuse of the text, at least they make committed efforts to read it and understand what it means for them. Significant numbers of conservatives will be found in one or more disciplined Bible study groups. The worldwide use of the Alpha Program originating in an evangelical Anglican church in London, or Rick Warren's books on the church and the Christian life are basic resources in thousands of conservative religious communities.[2] New Christians tend to be pushed hard to become literate about the Biblical text and to grow in their study of the "Word."

A loyalty to the work of the local congregation

Progressives are often astonished at the ability of evangelicals to massively support their congregations, as well as their larger missions. The obvious answer is a profound sense of stewardship. Among many evangelicals the tithe, and beyond, is a joyful expectation. Progressives tend to think of their relationship to the work of the church and its support as a voluntary activity.

A discovery of the importance of public life

Of late many evangelicals have come to realize that there is a clear relationship between the Christian faith and public affairs. The faith is not just about personal piety, getting into heaven or obeying religious laws. It has to do with every aspect of our common life, and that includes politics. The time is over when one would hear most evangelicals loudly disclaim any interest in what goes in the world beyond the walls of the church.

A growing concern for the left out

In recent years evangelicals have taken a renewed interest in the nobodies and the troubled in their communities. The only two groups I know about that have taken seriously the plight of addicts and alcoholics are Alcoholic Anonymous and conservative churches. A generation ago it was the liberals who were deeply involved in what we might call the social gospel. Now most conservative churches have vast programs geared to reach the dregs of society. While we may question the motivation, the compassion toward the homeless, single mothers, addicts of all sorts, and the poor is now deeply grounded in most evangelical churches. One is much more inclined to see a wide range of social, racial, and economic groups in evangelical churches than in most progressive churches.

A religion of the heart

Evangelicals are increasingly aware that the heart is as much a religious organ as the head. The emotions are not only evil forces to be controlled, but also vital aspects of faithful living. In worship people are free not just to lift their hands, but to dance, weep, shout, laugh, and embrace. An evangelical's ability to publicly testify to what God is doing in her/his life is a vital part of most services of worship. God is also to be praised with more than the intellect. God is loved with heart, soul, and strength as well as the mind.

An increased appreciation of the arts

Evangelicals are not afraid to take seriously the modern use of the arts.

Modern music, combined with contemporary celebrative worship styles, is a given. Evangelicals are able to learn new hymns and to adapt so-called secular music to church use. Organs, bulletins, printed prayers have given way to a more spontaneous present form of worship. Many large conservative congregations now have on their staffs a "Director of the Arts."

A passion to reach the young

Evangelicals tend to realize that the future of faith belongs to the young. While most major mainline denominations were busy cutting staffs and programs for young people and children, evangelicals were dramatically increasing resources in an effort to reach these groups. If liberal Christians look at the great sea of white hair in their shrinking churches, and ask where all the young people are, they just need to look across town at the latest charismatic tabernacle.

While there may be adequate reasons to raise questions about every one of the above evangelical activities and perspectives, nevertheless there are ways in which they make a contribution from which progressives might learn.

Notes

[1] Ephesians 5:21-6:9
[2] Warren Rick *The Purpose Driven Life* Zondervan, Grand Rapids, 2002 has consistently been on the best seller list ever since its publication

CHAPTER 5

Where the Evangelicals May Have Gone Wrong

We have suggested several values, styles and disciplines where conservative Christians may have it right. Nevertheless, significant numbers of these faithful folk have been seduced by a political system determined to use them for purposes having nothing to do with the Christian faith. This successful seduction constitutes an enormous problem, not only for the church of Jesus Christ, but also for United States, and even for the future, security, and well-being of the world.

Jan Linn has spelled out the heart of the problem in his book, *What's Wrong with the Christian Right.*[1] The cooptation of otherwise sincere Christians is an enormous and dangerous complex of issues. Many Christians have been massively taken in by an insidious and un-Christian philosophy with profound political implications. Consider a sampling of areas in which the Christian right may have it wrong.

When "Christian" only means evangelical

Many evangelicals assume that they are the only Christians, and that other so- called Christians are something less. They have been assisted in this takeover by the public media, which increasingly assumes that "Christian" means "right wing." Consider the following examples.

For a decade leaders of the progressive movement in the National Council of Churches have been working on a plan to enlarge the ecumenical Christian dialogue. For the first time Protestants, Catholics, and Orthodox have begun to explore what it might mean to walk together. The press reported, however, that "evangelicals have joined Catholics in new interchurch conversations." The implication is that Protestant means evangelical, and evangelical means the Christian right. That designation may be appropriate in Latin America where all Protestants are referred to as evangelicals, but it is not accurate when applied to Protestants in North America. But in the popular mind these days, Protestant tends to mean only the Christian right. Progressive Christians, who instigated the ecumenical discussions, are ignored.

Numbers of on-the-street conversations I have had reveal that when non-church people think of Christians these days, they usually mean "right wingers." Newspapers also reported that Christians (meaning evangelicals) swung the election in November 2004. In the popular mind all Christians now seem to be identified as belonging to the conservative camp. While progressives may stand on the sidelines, jump up and down and say, "Here we are. Look at us. We still count. We are also Christians," nobody seems to be paying attention. Radio and television religion tends to be almost entirely right wing. In most communities the large aggressive and thriving churches tend to be very conservative. When people are asked to name America's religious leaders, Jerry Falwell, Pat Robertson, James Dobson, Billy Graham, and occasionally Robert Schuller are the names commonly given. When they are asked to list significant progressive or liberal Christian leaders, there is most often a total silence. A scattering of progressives can name Spong, Borg, and a few others, but few members even of liberal churches can name anyone. Progressives, who at one time dominated the public square, are nowhere in sight. Their places have been occupied by Christians committed to a very different notion of faith and its societal implications.

Voting against your self-interest

So thoroughly has the Republican Party, now dominated by the neocons, hoodwinked otherwise sincere Christians, millions of good religious people have consistently voted both against their own self-interest as well as the clear implications of the Christian faith. A detailed version of this phenomenon can be found in a recent book that analyzes the voting patterns in Kansas.[2] People in that very Red State voted in massive numbers against their deeply held values and their economic interests.

During the months prior to the November 2004 election, I conducted a series of interviews with ordinary citizens of a middle-sized Midwestern city. I asked,

"What are the biggest problems in your life and the life of people who live around here?" I consistently got the same answers. Consider these responses:

"We can't afford the medicines we need. It's either food or pills, and we choose food."

"Our doctor's bills are beyond us, so we just quit going." It might be noted that about half of the bankruptcies in the United States are due to health-related expenses. The number of bankruptcies tripled from 1980 to 2001. Health-related bankruptcies increased twenty-three fold over the same period.[3]

"There are no jobs left in this community. We had five or six large employers in town, but the government has taken away our factories and shipped them overseas."

"We can get minimum wage jobs, but we can't live on what they pay."

"Members of my family live in fear of being homeless. Several people I know have lost their homes. Nobody thinks about the poor any more. The government lowers taxes on rich people, but who cares about us? The gap between them and us gets wider all the time. "

"There used to be strong unions in this city, but the politicians have helped destroy them."

"Social security is all we have. What will my kids live on if they gut the Social Security program?"

"Too many of our young people have been taken off to Iraq to fight a war we don't understand. At first I thought it was to safeguard America—all the talk about terrorism, weapons of mass destruction. But now I'm not so sure."

After this consistent litany of grievances, all of which constituted the substantial issues addressed in the Democratic platform and by Democratic candidates, I asked the question,

"Who are you going to vote for?" Among evangelical Christians the answer was consistent: "George Bush."

I responded, "Given what you say are the problems around here, how is it you are voting for a man and a Party whose policies oppose you at every turn?"

The answers to this question were also consistent 1-"George Bush is a born-again, God-fearing Christian man." 2-"He is opposed to gay marriage and abortion." These two issues seemed to be the only ones that mattered. Everything else was to be put aside. But if you look carefully, it will be clear that it was not a matter of *issues*, it was a matter of *values*. The facts didn't matter, only the appearance or what George Lakoff calls the "framing."[4]

Lakoff suggests that people are not set free by facts. The easy assumption is that most people are rational, and if you give them the truth they will come to thoughtful conclusions—and their conclusions will determine their voting patterns. But people do not think in terms of facts, says Lakoff, but in terms of frames. If the facts don't fit the frame, the frame will be the basis for decision making.[5] A frame is a large image that suggests a worldview. It may have little relationship to the facts, but points to a system of values. "Relief," for instance, implies a distress for which there can be a remedy. "Tax relief" suggests that taxes are painful, and to reduce them relieves the pain. The fact that most of the relief goes to the richest Americans is not the issue. Many people don't care about the facts. The notion—the frame—of relief itself captures their attention.[6]

Freedom, liberty, opportunity, morality, prosperity are all powerful framing words, regardless of the facts which lie behind them. To bring freedom to a nation by invading and occupying it, resulting in thousands of civilian deaths, is a case in point. The *framing* word is "freedom." The *fact* that the invasion and destruction of a nation is what happens, pales when put beside the word "freedom."[7] Evangelicals responded to very clever framing which had little to do with reality. In fact, many of the words used conveyed the opposite of the facts behind them.

A few examples: In order to do away with certain environmental directives, the Administration called the legislation, which allows increased industrial pollution, "The Clean Air Act." "Clean Air" is the framing word. Environmental disaster is the fact. The destruction of protected natural forests on behalf of the logging industry, was called, "The Healthy Forests Act." "Peace" meant war. Because these framing words were in the hands of someone they believed to be a born-again, God fearing Christian, the facts behind the words didn't matter.

World domination as a Christian principle

Remember how the neocons have been committed to a U.S. policy in which we essentially dominate not only the world but also outer space? Recall how this has been further spelled out in George W. Bush's official foreign policy statement, and in his January 2005 inaugural address. While there may be those evangelicals who accept wholesale that set of policies and want to see the United States rule the world by force of arms, many other conservative Christians are not at all committed to that disastrous philosophy. Their problem is that when they signed on to the Bush religious affirmation, they also almost automatically took on a political philosophy which came with the package. Having been lured into the political cave, they found inside a series of things they had not counted on. But now that they were in, there didn't seem any way either to get out or to be selective in what they accepted. They were default supporters of the war against Iraq, tax relief for the affluent, the widening of the discrepancy between rich and poor, world domination by force of arms, the tearing of the social welfare net, the despoiling of the natural environment for the sake of profits—on and on and on, because Bush, a good Christian man, believed in these things.

How is it that so many solid religious people have bought this disastrous and un-Christian package? I can only conclude that they have been seduced. What they bought is not what they assumed came with an anti-same-sex marriage and an anti-abortion agenda—matters about which Jesus had nothing to say.

There may be otherwise sincere Christians who accept the entire package. These things are what they really believe. Dialogue, or any attempt to reason with them, is probably futile. But there are others, I believe many others, who do not accept the contents of the package, but don't know how to get out of what they don't know how they got into.

Late in 2006, however, there appeared to be a series of fissures developing in a previously solid wall of support for the policies of a conservative political administration. It began as numbers of evangelical Christians began to look seriously at the slow destruction of the environment, particularly through global warming. In addition, with the increasingly unpopularity of the Iraqi war, other evangelicals were moved to take another look.

Are Christians up for sale?

Can Christians be easily bought? The relationship between a government that wants the support of a particular constituency, and the desire of that constituency to get what it needs from government, is an old story. Politicians consistently use their ability to deliver money, projects, and federal facilities to areas and groups to whom they then look for election-day support. President Bush's "Faith-Based Initiative" program is a continuation of a long-standing policy in which the government funds community projects operated by churches or religious associations. The congregation I served in Missouri built 57 apartment units on its property using a government guaranteed loan. Most of the units were designed for low-income residents who were to be assisted by the Federal Section 8 housing supplement.

Our city, as did most American communities, operated an interchurch nutrition program using USDA commodities. At no time, however, did a particular Administration remotely suggest these programs were either political payoffs or a way to secure votes. Few of us even remembered which Administration established any of the myriad programs in which the government assisted religious groups to engage in social service work.

Bush's Faith-Based Initiative program is of a somewhat different sort. The front page of the January 28, 2005 Los Angeles Times carries the tongue-in-cheek headline "Bush Rewarded by Black Pastor's Faith." The minister in question had been a longtime supporter of the Democratic Party and its major concerns. Now his picture had appeared on leaflets all the way to Wisconsin supporting the political campaign of George W. Bush. It turns out that his California congregation had, prior to the 2004 campaign, received a million and a half dollars for their community programs. In 2003 over a billion dollars was similarly spread around to religious groups, most of them from conservative churches. According to the Times, this program was devised by Carl Rove as part of a political strategy. While the President refused to see a delegation of United Methodist Bishops—Bush is a United Methodist—groups of conservative pastors, Black and White, have enjoyed White House invitations. A series of meetings of African American pastors has been held across the country in an effort to solidify the relationship between conservative Black Christians and the Administration. High on the agenda of these meetings was solid opposition to same-sex marriages. Jesse Jackson once asked a large group of Black pastors how many of them have been asked to perform a same-sex marriage. There were no hands. But the issue remains a hot button.

The combination of dollars given and the same-sex issue has worked for the President. The percentage of African Americans in the Republican column rose substantially in the 2004 election. These votes typically came from prominent African American churches. As we approach the 2008 elections, however, that support seems to be seriously waning. Support by African American Christians may not be that easily bought.

Beyond national politics, conservative religious leaders, having reaped the largess of the Administration's financial blessings, have been hard at work taking control of State and local political organizations. The March 27, 2005 New York Times described how Ohio pastors, black and white, had launched a campaign to win control of both local governmental posts and State offices. "Patriot Pastors" are committed to register a million God-fearing voters in that State. Once the political juggernaut of Ohio's fundamentalists got rolling, even leaders of the traditional conservative Republican Party viewed the development with alarm.

One cannot fault the Administration for using these tactics. Carl Rove and crew need to be respected for their sagacity and political wisdom. The question, however, is whether the recipients of this largess have simply been seduced by Bush's pot of gold. The issue is theological more than it is political.

The question of Christian values

Probably the one most potent issue in the 2004 election centered around the word "values." Evangelicals voted in significant numbers for what they held to be Christian values. When asked to define what Christian values actually were, the predominant response had to do with sexual matters, namely same-sex marriage and abortion. Since George W. Bush took clear positions on these issues, he won the values debate hands down. In the next chapter we will take a closer look at both these issues, but for now we need to step back from them and look at the matter of Christian values more broadly.

There is no question that the question of values is central to the Christian affirmation, and to the political life which flows from it. The matter of values is a profound theological concern to all those who call Jesus their Lord. Jesus' ministry was grounded in a values agenda. The Commonwealth of God he proclaimed was centered in the values question. It is important, therefore to examine the issues to which Jesus bore positive witness.

In explaining the teachings of Jesus a generation or two after his death, a Jewish-Christian, who was probably the leader of what we know as the Matthean community, authored a collection of Jesus' most important sayings popularly known as, "The Sermon on the Mount." The values which are explicit in this collection include poverty of spirit, mourning, meekness, mercy, purity of heart, hunger and thirst for righteousness, and peacemaking. Luke, looking at the same collection de-spiritualizes much of it and states that the poor and the hungry are particularly blessed people. The rich and the full were those who felt Jesus' scorn.

Matthew goes on to talk about sexual purity, particularly about adultery, divorce, and oaths. He then moves to harder issues such as retaliation—which he claimed Jesus abjured—and loving one's enemies. There followed notions about the danger of riches and judging others.

Luke has Jesus announce the content and purpose of his ministry as similar human matters. Jesus' self-identified mission consisted of: good news to the poor, release to the captive, sight to the blind, and liberty to the oppressed. This was to be accomplished through the activation of the Jewish notion of the year of Jubilee—the time of God's favor.

While much of the gospel deals with charity and benevolence, justice is an underlying theme. According to Reinhold Niebuhr, justice is what love means when it is in the plural. "Justice is the legal tender of love." Substantial to the gospels is a concern for issues of justice, poverty, the left out and despised, love of one's enemies, judging others, and similar matters. These themes are consistently affirmed not only in the Gospels, but also in the rest of the New Testament.

Once in a seminary preaching class, a student, given to the power of the homiletic demonstration, took a pair of scissors to his New Testament and cut out every passage that referred to the poor, the left out, the non-persons, the strangers, the foreigners and the oppressed, and how God would have them treated. He held up a much thinner and tattered Bible and challenged his fellow students to cut from their Bibles every text that had to do with abortion. While the demonstration might have been a bit strained, the point was clear. When Jesus talked about values, they had to do with how we treat enemies, how we serve the poor, how we bring equality to human life, and to a long series of similar issues.

The relationship between mercy and judgment, however, is to be taken seriously. Reinhold Niebuhr helped the Christian world understand that while Jesus defined the Reign of God as committed to justice, peace, and equity, he also took head-on the presence of evil and the need to confront it. Pacifism might well be a thoroughly righteous perspective. However, according to Niebuhr, Christian faith could not always be reduced to turning the other cheek and going the second mile. There are times when evil must be confronted. Nevertheless, the Christian gospel leans toward non-violence, forgiveness and the strength of reconciliation. I have never been an advocate of bumper stickers, but I do carry one on the back of my car. It reads, "WHEN JESUS SAID, 'LOVE YOUR ENEMIES', I DON'T THINK HE MEANT THAT WE SHOULD KILL THEM."

Values are just theoretical concerns until they appear spelled out in public policies, and this is where values and politics intersect. Joan Chittister put it this way: "National budgets are a nation's theology walking!" Martin Luther King said, "The arc of history bends toward justice." That's the essence of Christian politics.

There are certain themes repeated over and over again throughout the Bible. They are not peripheral or subsidiary. They are central to Christian faith in every time and in every place. They are the substance of Jesus' life and teachings. They are the evidences that the Reign of God has come near. There is a clear presumption in the Bible and in Christian history that Christian faith is against war and for human equality and universal dignity. The post Vatican II Bishops of Latin America were right when they declared that God had a preferential option for the poor. Therefore, they posited that the church must evidence that same preference. The question of values, therefore, centers on what is central to the life and teachings of Jesus and of his church when it has been at its best. Three billion of the world's people living on less than 2 dollars a day is a profound religious issue!

Moreover, it is clear in Jesus' ethic that no one was to be seen as an outsider, a non-person, the other. The only persons who fell under Jesus' judgment were those who thought themselves to be the insiders and others the outsiders—"who trusted in themselves that they were righteous, and despised others."

Much of the religious right has simply ignored the ethical or values substance Jesus demonstrated. Since these matters seem today to fall outside the orbit of conservative politics—indeed are resisted at practically every turn, we must conclude that those who ignore them seriously distort and misidentify the relationship between Christian faith and political policies and action.

Notes

[1] Linn, Jan G. *What's Wrong with the Christian Right* Brown Walker Press Boca Raton 2004.

If you are looking for a careful evaluation of where the evangelical church has missed the point, check out Linn's thorough analysis.

[2] Frank, Thomas *What's the Matter with Kansas* Henry Holt and Company New York 2004.

[3] Los Angeles Times February 2, 2005.

[4] Lakoff, George *don't think of an elephant* Chelsea Green Publishing White River Junction 2004.

[5] Ibid p. 17.

[6] Ibid p. 9.

[7] Ibid p. 13.

CHAPTER 6

Issues Vital to Evangelicals

Many sincere evangelicals see a pair of moral issues as vital to the sanctity of life. One concern seeks to protect the unborn. The other seeks to protect the institution of marriage. It is important that progressives realize the depth of passion these two matters have generated. Progressives also need to be able to state what they believe evangelicals think about these issues in terms religious conservatives are able to say, "Yes, that is what we believe." To attack someone else's point of view without first understanding it or being able to articulate it in terms the other accepts cannot lead to any common understanding or resolution.

Abortion

Devout conservatives believe that human life begins at conception. This is true both in Catholic moral theology and in the less systematized Protestant ethical understanding.

Here is what I conclude most evangelicals sincerely believe. The product of conception, at that moment, is not an undifferentiated bit of organic matter. It is a human being, with all the rights which adhere to any person. Therefore, to terminate that life is morally akin to murder, notwithstanding the Supreme Court or any legislative perspective.

The fact that at various times in religious history there have been other notions of when life begins is beside the point. The proposition that there is no human life until quickening, or when the baby is able to survive outside the womb, denies the conviction a mother normally has even at the earliest weeks of pregnancy. She probably thinks of the life within her as a person, her baby, not just a fetus. A friend of mine faced that reality when he observed the ultrasound image of the twin girls his wife was carrying. "They were my daughters—persons just as much our babies as they were at birth, or even now on their third birthday." Technology has altered the more primitive way people thought about the when human life actually begins.

No argument, not even the rights of the mother to control her own body, has the emotional power of this more conservative conclusion. Those of us who hold to a "pro-choice" position on the subject cannot simply dismiss this deeply held conviction by the "pro-life" community.

It is doubtful that those of us on different sides of this issue will ever come to the position where we all agree. That implies somebody would have to undergo radical changes of mind and heart, and I doubt that is going to be a happen anytime soon—or ever. Yet, it is time to stop shouting at each other across picket lines. Those things, which only harden the perspectives, will not lead to an intelligent settlement of the matter.

Is there then another way to think together about this vital issue? Are there areas where we can agree, without having to dramatically renounce long-held positions? Can we agree, for instance, that abortion is most often a less than desirable compromise when faced with an unanticipated or unwanted pregnancy? Can we agree that when the life or health of the mother is at risk, there may be room to consider termination of a pregnancy? Can we agree that every pregnant couple must consider all the options available to them when they are faced with an unwanted pregnancy? Raising the child as a single parent, adoption, marriage, raising the child as a married or unmarried couple, or raising the child as part of an extended family or clan ought always be part of the conversation. Finally, can we agree that the best possible solution is to find ways to minimize abortions, realizing that there will always be either legal or non-legal remedies in cases of unwanted pregnancies? If we can begin with these presuppositions, then we can look together at those things that produce unwanted pregnancies and thus abortions, and those things that prevent them.

Obviously we must start with adequate birth control. Any policy which prohibits the availability and use of condoms, other devices, or pills available to restrict pregnancy promotes abortion. In places and among religious people where birth control is denied, there will be a plethora of unwanted pregnancies and therefore medical terminations. Politicians who cut from budgets the availability of appropriate birth control devices or who gut programs if the recipients include birth control as part of their program, perpetuate the high level of abortions.

Any Administration's "pro-life" policy, which withholds funds from international planning bodies and limits family planning services, has directly increased the number of terminations.

Can we further agree that abstinence may not be a bad word?

Legal sanctions do no cut abortion rates. In Belgium and the Netherlands, where abortion is both legal and covered under a national health plan, the rate of abortions is the lowest of any place in the world—seven per 1,000 women of child-bearing age. In nations such as Peru and Brazil, where abortion is prohibited by law, the rate is about 50 per 1,000 women of child-bearing age. In the United States the rate is about 22.[1]

It is also clear that abortion rates go down when the economic condition of the marginalized goes up. When there are ways by which a community has rallied to raise a child—perhaps an entire village—there is less need for artificial termination of pregnancies. When the social safety net is strong, abortion rates plummet. When the social safety net is in tatters, abortion rates climb dramatically. Termination rates went down during the years of the Clinton Administration. During the first Bush term, rates went back up. The variable seems to coincide with the availability and funding of supportive structures in the community. At the same time, to require "work instead of welfare" offers many poor women and families little option other than to eliminate just one more potential family member.

The evidence is clear. The criminalization of abortion doesn't solve the problem or decrease the number or rate of terminations. Therefore, those who are serious about wanting as few abortions in society as possible cannot rely on the overturning of Roe v. Wade or any other legislative or judicial remedy to solve the problem. A just society in which the need of abortions is dramatically reduced is a direction that both pro-life and pro-choice advocates might well consider. If, however, as many claim, this is a deeply felt moral matter, then the answer may be to make abortion unconscionable, not illegal.

Same-sex marriage

The second issue about which many evangelicals hold intense feelings concerns homosexuality, particularly the matter of same-sex marriage. Conservatives do not see homosexuality as an alternative lifestyle, and many view it as a sin. The claim is that the Bible both authorizes and sanctifies marriage as a sacrament between one man and one woman, and condemns sexual relationships between any two people of the same sex. The overwhelming fear is that the institution of marriage and the sanctity of the family are at stake. The claim is that allowing this very different understanding of marriage compromises the integrity of the institution. In the American South, as well as in other parts of the nation, the family unit is the glue that holds society accountable. It has been the family unit that made the small farm viable. A community is commonly thought to be a collection of traditional families.

In many places, the family was held together by a strong father, who was not only the breadwinner but also the moral authority and head of the house. The hierarchy in family life proceeded from father to mother to children. Same-sex marriage is said to abrogate this historic inner-family relationship. What is more, if the family is the unit of procreation, same-sex marriages are unable to fulfill this pattern except by artificial insemination or adoption. Conservatives feel that healthy children need both a resident father and a resident mother to properly grow into maturity.

Conservatives cite a well-known collection of seven Biblical texts, which seem to condemn sex between persons of the same gender. To ignore the violation specified in these passages, they believe, is an abomination in the eyes of God. Homosexuality is seen as unnatural, and to violate the laws of nature is to violate the laws of God.

So there are three main issues about which conservatives tend to focus their attention regarding same-sex marriage: the Biblical injunction against sex between persons of the same gender, the preservation of the institution of the traditional family, and the dominant position of the senior male as head of the house.

Those in the progressive camp are well aware of the arguments on the other side. Good Biblical scholarship casts these seven texts in a very different light. There have been scores of family constellations, in Biblical literature and beyond that in no way mirror what many assume is the traditional nuclear family. In many places today the majority of members of a church or a community do not live in traditional nuclear families. The reality for many gay and lesbian persons is that their sexual orientation is their God-given nature, and to violate their nature is to violate God's gift. Evidence abounds that healthy children are produced and raised in homes where there are two mothers or two fathers, without injury to the little ones. There is no evidence that same-sex couples in a community compromise the traditional family structures at any point. No family is injured because down the street from its house is a family with two mothers or two fathers. The legal denial of marriage is a denial of the legal rights of gay and lesbian persons, and the denial of legal rights to gay and lesbian people is the great civil rights struggle the nation is now called upon to address.

At this point it is not our purpose to defend or argue for any of these divergent propositions. We accept the fact that sincere and devout persons will differ in how they handle or what they think about this constellation of issues. What is important is that those on either side of this divide are able to articulate the position of the other in terms about which the other can say, "yes, that's what we believe." The question for us is whether there are places of agreement that do not deny the validity or the right of those on opposite sides to hold their opinions.

Again let's examine a series of questions that may lead to some resolution of the conflict:

- Can we agree that marriage is fundamentally a way in which the religious institution either blesses or

withholds blessing on relationships between two persons?
- Can we agree that no government can require any religious institution to join in marriage those it deems unfit?
- Can we agree that under the Constitution and laws of the United States, no persons can be denied the civil rights granted to every person?
- Do positive responses to these questions on both sides give us a platform to meet a great variety of opinions without compromising important basic concerns held by those in a variety of camps?

The questions may hinge on whether marriage is viewed as a religious moral commitment between two persons, or only a legal arrangement sanctioned by the State. Is the clergy person performing a wedding ceremony simply an agent of the government, or is marriage grounded in a covenant before God by two persons? When I perform a wedding, is it my role to do so "on behalf of the State of California," or "as a priest of God"?

Tony Campolo and Jim Wallis, both significant evangelical leaders, suggest that marriage is too sacred to be reduced to a civil function. On the other hand, those who choose to live together and share all the legal requirements and privileges the State has a right to grant should be entitled to enter into a binding legal agreement with or without religious sanction. [2]

Persons either of the same gender of different genders wishing to enter such a legal arrangement might apply to the proper legal authority for a contract which becomes binding on them and on the legal structures of society.

Those wishing a religious solemnization of marriage would ask their particular religious community to bless their relationship. As noted, no religious institution is under any obligation to bless that which it does not believe it can bless. Increasingly some churches and synagogues are welcoming same-sex couples and celebrating with them their commitment to each other. Other religious bodies believe that the marriage of same-sex couples is contrary to their basic beliefs and will not perform the rites of marriage. Either way, this is not just a legal arrangement, but a profoundly religious one.

This solution may meet the needs of a great variety of differing perspectives. Religious institutions are protected from having to bless that which they think is un-blessable. The State leaves the moral questions to the church and concerns itself only with the legal rights and responsibilities of two persons who choose to enter into a contract. Under the law there is the elimination of two classes of persons—the married and those who have only a civil arrangement. While these two classes of persons might have equal rights, we are several decades beyond realizing that "separate but equal" is an unjustifiable doctrine in matters of race, and now in matters pertaining to gender orientation. Before the law everyone gets the same treatment and is offered the same contract.

Any proposed Constitutional amendment sinks the government ever more deeply into the religious world. On the other hand, if the word "marriage" is devoid of religious meaning and is only a purely secular arrangement, then secularists will face the emotional conflict that comes in recognizing that what they have called marriage is really only a legal contract.

Solutions surrounding these two significant moral issues, abortion and same-sex marriage, cannot revolve around who is going to win the argument. Ways must be identified in which those of widely differing perspective are respected without forcing their irreconcilable opinions on others. Unless we can come to some solution to these important matters, there will be a long and unhappy perpetuation of the culture wars, which really revolve around deeply held religious commitments. If, however, there is some resolution, those who have found political advantage in the perpetuation of the conflict will lose these political weapons.

Notes

[1] These statistics were reported in *The Christian Century*, February 22, 2005.

[2] This perspective has been outlined by Jim Wallis in *God's Politics* Harper San Francisco 2004 p. 304ff.

CHAPTER 7

The Distressing Retreat of the Liberal Church

Jim Wallis holds that while the evangelicals may have gotten it wrong, liberal Christians just don't get it. Wallis and other "progressive evangelicals" go to great lengths to illustrate the first thesis, but are far less clear on the details of the second. What does it mean that liberal Christians don't get it? Even while there is a paucity of crisp analyses in Wallis and others, it is clear that the fall of mainline Christian religion goes far deeper than its numerical loses. Critiques of the National Council of Churches and those denominations which are part of it abound. Attacks by the leaders of the right wing group, including the late Jerry Falwell, Pat Robertson, and James Dobson are encyclopedic. But one hardly finds an objective analysis by those who are licking their lips over the problems faced by every mainline denomination.

The fact that evangelical churches are growing and liberal ones declining says little about the validity of those two now very different sorts of religious enterprises. Unrestrained growths may just be malignancies. When Henry David Thoreau was asked what he thought about the new railroad that was being built near Walden Pond, he responded, "It just may be evil going faster." Growth may be one sign of faithfulness, but it is not the only sign, and certainly not the most dependable sign. Places in the world, and times where a single fundamentalist religion has dominated the scene, have often turned out to be far removed from anything remotely resembling the ethical imperative proclaimed by Jesus as constituting the Commonwealth of God.

Even so, the disastrous decline of traditional denominations needs to be taken seriously. Every year leaders tell us that things have finally "bottomed out." But the following year they say the same thing. I doubt if as yet we are near the bottom.

The conservative assault on progressive churches

The United Methodist Church provides an example of the adverse relationship between right-wing religion and the problems of mainline churches. This, once the largest American Protestant body, is losing thousands of members every year. What is more, it is currently under severe assault by a vigorous conservative constituency. As has been the case within Methodism before, the upshot may well be a split resulting in at least one new conservative denomination. When the chips are on the table, conservatives often don't even agree with each other. Indeed, every time the Methodist Church added a required year of education for its clergy, it peeled from the soft cultural underbelly of the body yet another denomination or two. Consider the Nazarenes, the Wesleyan Methodists, the African Methodist Episcopal Church—not to mention the major division, now healed, that occurred at the time of the Civil War.

The current internal struggle, however, is different. The attack on the United Methodists is being financed by forces outside the denomination. The Good News organization of the United Methodist Church is made up of conservative persons who are committed to reforming the Church or leaving it, en masse. They are part of a network of similar bodies inside most major denominations. Many of these groups are connected to and funded by the right-wing Institute for Religion and Democracy. It ought to come as no surprise that the major issues of these groups are focused around homosexuality and abortion. The theological cover for these, and other mostly sexual matters, is defended as faithfulness to the Bible.

The IRD is tied, by virtue of the donors who fund it liberally, to conservative Republican sources. In many cases right-wing political operators have infiltrated where they can and used their massive influence to disrupt otherwise progressive church structures. Most ordinary parishioners are probably unaware where the funds come from that continue to disrupt mainline congregations and their denominational agencies. A significant amount of IRD funding is generated from sources not even remotely connected with the Christian tradition. An already weakened United Methodist Church is having to spend too much of its depleted resources fighting a rear-guard action against those who have probably been seduced without even knowing it.[1]

It is not our purpose here to delve into the various diseases of mainline religion. That set of difficulties has been spelled out sufficiently in a shelf of books that have attempted to analyze the malaise. Three of these books bear my name.[2] Our point here is that the same political forces that have managed to seduce so many right-wing Christians have also used money and influence to exacerbate the decline of mainline churches.

Progressive religion's retreat

While the Christian right has been responsible for part of the decline of liberal denominations, the basic responsibility for their demise rests with the liberals themselves, not some outside source. While it is true that throughout the mainline establishment there has been a steady erosion of members, it should not be assumed that most of these people have gravitated to a local tabernacle or other conservative church. Significant numbers have simply opted out of church life altogether. Whatever was going on in their former congregations, it was not meeting many of their needs.

Efforts to stem the hemorrhaging have proved largely unsuccessful. It has often been like struggling to get loose from a straight jacket. The harder you try, the tighter the straps. I have consulted with a number of shrinking congregations that have attempted to solve their problem by making certain nothing is said anywhere in the church that could offend the conservative members. I have talked to a number of ministers who were clearly on the progressive side of church life and Christian theology. But they are mute. Why? Because significant numbers of their members are not only born-again adherents of the Christian right, but are also among the congregation's substantial givers. "I've already lost a lot of people, and I can't afford to lose any more. So I've got to be very careful what I say." In community-wide meetings of progressives called to think through the implications of the current set of problems, these ministers don't ever show up, lest somebody report their presence.

Many ministers and other progressive church leaders, feel their role is limited to trying to keep people as happy as possible. Thus the proliferation of soft, harmless programs for "all ages and interests." "My job," several ministers have reported, "is pastoral. I am here to take care of my people. To offend them would be outside my call." What is lost is courage! It may be too much to ask many of our abused clergy and their decimated congregations to position themselves as part of a prophetic minority. But to take no position and simply succumb to the mentality of the religious right—or seek to copy it—may be to deny important aspects of Christian faith.

In part the problem is institutional, and the self-identified job of the minister is often limited to keeping the institutional structure as sturdy as possible. So, many ministers have been reduced to becoming managers of small, struggling businesses. What is lost is their role as resident theologians. Having abdicated that task, many of their members have sought out other theologians and followed them. And who might these outside theologians be? Try Pat Robertson, James Dobson, and Jerry Falwell—or any one of a host of evangelists regularly seen on the Trinity Broadcast Network. Mark it down. If the minister is not the theologian in residence, someone else will be. When I have inquired as to how much time and effort ministers put into doing serious Bible study or theological training in the congregation, there is almost a universal denial that they have the time, background, or inclination for that sort of thing.

I have encountered several alert and responsive pastors who do believe part of their call is to be resident theologians, but who tell me that their schedule limits that aspect of their ministry to sermons. Certainly the pulpit is a vital avenue for theological instruction. However, one person talking and everybody else sitting in neutral, drifting in and out, is perhaps the least effective teaching modality to deal with critical issues presented by Christian faith. Preaching is still important. It may provide the only time many Christians hear the gospel and its implications for the world. People can be introduced to the good news of God's work in the world and God's will for the world, but the pulpit can only serve as the introduction. Having shown people the door to Christian maturity, they then must be helped to open it.

Toward a recovery of theology

When active in parish life, I spent significant time every week in a variety of in-depth theological studies with church members. It was expected that congregants participate in these sessions. This was particularly true for young or new Christians. I have discovered that this ministerial role is the exception, not the rule. On more than one occasion ministers of substantial congregations have told me that the reason no such classes exists in their churches is because "nobody is interested." A cluttered church social program just won't allow it.

Beyond the classroom, training in Christian maturity can take place utilizing a variety of action/reflection models. Few things are more valuable in teaching theology than the mission trip. Young people and adults have gone to some remote spot in the world to build a house, or an outhouse, and come back with a fresh understanding of the world and of the relationship between Christian faith and survival for the left out. The mission trip is most effective when it is accompanied by serious reflection on the relationship between the focus of the mission and the implications of the Christian faith. This peripatetic methodology is precisely the model Jesus used. He taught "on the way." If the congregation's budget is tight, and there is forced a decision between funding the choir for the year and sending the youth group to a Mexican village for a week, let the choir take a well-deserved Sabbatical.

Mission trips don't need to be to some far-away place. Every community holds opportunities for both compassionate and justice oriented encounters. The secret is to combine activity and reflection. First, the action. Then the reflection, which interprets the action.³ Both liberation theology and plain common sense are clear that this mode of teaching/learning is far superior to the sit-in-the-classroom-and-listen mode.

While we suggest that the essential problem with the Progressive church is theological, we do not mean there is not enough teaching about doctrine, or even not enough Bible study. Often congregational Bible study involves little more than groups of the saints who meet regularly to jump up and down on ten verses and come out about where they went in.

The recovery of courage in the congregation

The theological issue really goes to the question of moral substance. What is it we really believe? What is at the heart of our faith? What are the clear imperatives of the Christian gospel seen through the life and teachings of Jesus? The Progressive church has not only lost the high ground, it is often unclear that we stand on anything solid.

There is more involved than taking positions on a few social issues. Of course we ought to continue to speak out against unilateral invasions and a unipolar view of a world dominated by American power. Gay rights, care of the poor, and environmental protection will still consume our attention. But those things are symptoms of the deeper issues. Garret Keizer puts it this way:

> It does mean that a truly progressive agenda has to consist of something more radical than reminding the minimum-wage custodian to sort the recyclables when he takes out the trash, or the Latina housemaid to dust Che's portrait when she does the den. It might mean that we have to relinquish more of our disposable incomes in order to reduce the number of disposable people.[4]

While progressives continue to be alarmed at their shrinking constituencies, the reversion to church growth techniques may detract us from the central issues of our faith. Lewis Mudge put it this way: "If the churches are to play any worthwhile role in the world, they must first reclaim their calling to be distinctive, morally formative communities.... (they) need to become communities of disciplined moral life if they expect to make any serious impact on our time."[5]

We are called to generate communities that help reshape the world in which we all live, through the stories and actions that are told and retold about God's will for all God's creation and its creatures. We may do many other things; hold dandy dinners, rent buses for bluegrass concerts, put on fashion shows, and a thousand other pleasant activities one finds listed in church newsletters these days. But the heart of our calling is personal and social transformation through the story of Jesus of Nazareth and those who became his disciples. This is our moral imperative seen in terms of congregational action.

When we do take this matter seriously, often we are reduced to reporting the facts that prove our side of a political or social argument. We hear lectures about the statistics surrounding the war against Iraq, or the nature of global warming, or the control of space by military design. Or we may sit and watch another movie about how bad *they* are. While facts and erudite lectures may motivate a few people, they often do not generate the discipline it takes to build solid constituencies. Jack Jackson, the 2004-5 Moderator of the United Church of Christ, put it this way: "The mainline denominations have failed to develop a constituency within their membership which welcomed prophetic protest, or be receptive to a new vision." The temptation is to sit quietly in the center of the road and be run over by mega-trucks barreling down the right side of the highway.

The recovery of courage by the denominations

At denominational levels it is more than passing appropriate resolutions supporting good causes. It involves restructuring denominational budgets and goals so that the fundamental purpose of the body is to demonstrate what Jesus talked about from the first of his ministry to the last—the presence in history of the Reign of God. The core question every aspect and level of church must ask is this: Does who we are and what we profess demonstrate God's reign? Everything the church does must be subject to a holy triage. Religious dilettantes, who take few things seriously and are terribly afraid even to discuss the central questions of faith, are increasingly useless. Churches which operate under the rubric of the least common denominator cannot and do not evidence God's Reign. It might be this and it might be that—"ask not, tell not and it doesn't really matter," is no longer good enough, if it ever was.

Preemptive war, the continued mal-distribution of the world's resources, the shredding of the social safety net, a unipolar internationalist approach, the bypassing of the United Nations, the thumbing of the nose at treaties, the torture of prisoners of wars—now called enemy combatants—the denial of the prophets for the sake of profits, the continued development of new stronger nuclear weapons and a host of other issues are not just politically in error, they are morally repugnant, and the church needs to say so.

The way Christians face the world is essentially rooted in values. But when the values question is limited to abortion and homosexuality, we may be faced with the classic pharisaic dilemma—straining gnats and swallowing camels. Progressives seem to have temporarily lost the argument over values. But the profound values important to Christians, to the world and to the world's God are at the heart of what we believe and that to which we are called to bear courageous witness.

These issues are not limited to the church in the United States. As I have talked to sensitive Australians, and watch the Australian press, I ask myself the question which I believe is at the heart of the problem of the Progressive religious community: Where is the church? Hugh Mackay, in his March 25, 2005 column of *The Age*, the leading Australian newspaper, wrote, "The tragedy of Christianity is that its luminous ideas have been easily swept aside by the political, economic and cultural imperatives of institutional religion with its emphasis on hierarchy, power and self-protection."

He goes on, "And that is why so many Australians have distanced themselves from the institutional church. Many of the people who yearn for a more meaningful and fulfilling life would regard the church as an unlikely place to go for guidance."

Perhaps the problem is not that the Christian right has pre-empted the question of values, but that the progressive church has simply abdicated. We will never win back the eyes and ears of the world, or make the slightest impression on our sisters and brothers who have drifted almost out of sight of the gospel, as long as we are not clear about the world changing implications of our faith.

For the progressive church to restructure its life so that its moral agenda is lived out will be costly. It will mean giving up much that has been of value. It will mean being seen as an enemy by those who have a vested interest in the disturbing agenda now controlling our nation. Pastors will lose their jobs. Congregations may continue to shrink. Churches at every level will be forced to reevaluate their priorities. Those unwilling to pay the price may need to find alternative religious clubs that continue to sing them to sleep.

Such is the cost, which comes when any church decides to become a moral community, clear about the Christian faith and clear about the grace, acceptance and commission of God.

In the concluding chapters we will be examining a series of practical suggestions on how individuals, congregations, denominations, progressive interfaith associations and non-religious community groups might develop specific plans to take back the territory from the neocons who have seduced many of us.

Notes

[1] The relationship between Republican money sources and the Institute for Religion and Democracy, which has been pivotal in the attack on the United Methodist Church and other mainline denominations, is well documented in "Special Report—Follow the Money," which appeared in the July/August 2003 edition of *Zion's Herald*, a journal of the United Methodist Church.

[2] *The Babylonian Captivity of the Mainline Church* Chalice Press St. Louis 1996
Hope for the Mainline Church CBP Press 1991
A Resurrected Church Chalice Press 2001

[3] I have developed a rather extensive plan for this action/reflection theological training program. See Charles Bayer *Connect—Faith in Action* Living Bread Press, St. Louis 2003.

[4] Garret Keizer, writing in MOTHER JONES March-April 2005 p.44

[5] Mudge, Lewis S. *The Church as Moral Community* Continuum, New York 1998

CHAPTER 8

Re-visioning the Progressive Church

Any effort to reclaim significant sectors of the seduced evangelical church must begin with America's progressive Christian community. Liberal Christianity largely abandoned the field a few years ago. This abdication was a hesitant reaction to its persistent numerical decline, which began in the 1970s and continues to this day. This phenomenon has been widely discussed in a shelf of books. The roots of the problem are complex. The essence of the matter may lie in the death of Christendom. I have dealt with this demise at some length in my book *The Resurrected Church*, Chalice Press, St. Louis, 2001.

On the margins—the church's proper place

As I suggested in that book, the hunger for success, for popularity and for numeric hegemony may historically have been the downfall of the Christian enterprise. It is possible that our current loss of centrality in the public square may be a gift of God calling us back to Biblical authenticity. The Christian enterprise may well be best positioned on the margins, not the center. That is where Jesus lived. That was the background of his first followers. That is how the early church was understood by Jews, Romans, and Greeks. John Updike put it this way: "There is a way in which success disagrees with Christianity, and its proper venue is embattlement—a furtive hanging on in the catacombs, or at ill-attended services in dying rural and inner-city parishes. Its perilous, marginal, mocked existence serves as an image or our own, beneath whatever appearances of success is momentarily mustered."

A church looking to recapture Christendom is facing in the wrong direction. By Christendom we mean a cultural domination by the church: its language, ethic, political alliances, artistic expressions, philosophic constructs, and social contracts. This domination began with Constantine and grew in power throughout much of western history. Our era, however, has witnessed a continual diminution of this ecclesial hegemony. While founded as a nation committed to the non-establishment of religion, nevertheless, the Colonies and the early days of the American republic were shot through with Christian references and Christian expressions. While we rejected the notion of an official State religion, we continued to cling to many of the ethical imperatives authentic Christian faith had long held to be politically precious.

As I have earlier noted, the ethos of much of the American South, as well as other parts of the heartland, assumed that the Christian faith, basically traditional Protestantism, was inseparable from the nature of public life. While Church and State were officially distinguished by Madison's Wall of Separation, American life was replete with religious symbolism and institutional sanctions. Protestant hegemony was still in place well through the first half of the 20th century.

When I was a Junior High School student in the suburbs of Philadelphia, each class day at this public school was begun with a reading from the Bible and a short prayer. A full-blown Christian chapel service was conducted weekly by the school's principal. Christmas and Easter were clearly religious holidays, and crèches appeared on City Hall lawns. Copies of the Ten Commandments, in print and occasionally in stone, were displayed in classrooms, courthouses, and a variety of other public places. Football games began with prayer, as did—and still does—the daily opening of Congress. While there was no formally established church in the United States, the informal establishment of Protestantism was unmistakable. The election of a non-Protestant President was unthinkable. Al Smith didn't make it, and the nomination of JFK filled many Protestants with horror. It would not be long, they felt, until the Pope moved his headquarters to Pennsylvania Avenue.

As new legal suits were brought and the courts increasingly compromised these practices across the country, the cry arose from the religious conservatives, "God has been taken out of our schools." It had become increasingly obvious that the quasi-formal link between church and state could not stand the light of investigation, and the courts issued a series of rulings to the contrary. Nevertheless, evangelicals were horrified. "This is a Christian nation," they cried, "founded on the Word of God, and no pagan Court is going to change it."

If many progressive—then called liberal—Christians shared the horror of this disestablishment, their ecclesial leaders tended to be generally more comfortable with the gradual changes. But down in the trenches of even the most progressive churches, there was an ominous rumbling and numbers of the disaffected grew. The temptation was to seek again the cultural domination inherent in Christendom. Many liberals hold the nostalgic notion that they can again become central players in American culture—taking it back again from the evangelicals, who now seem to have a lock on this social position. But Christendom is dead, and authentic Christian faithful are ill-advised to try and resurrect it. Progressives must learn to operate from the margins, not from the center of society. Fundamentalism's quest for centrality is not only bad Christian faith, it is bad public policy.

The evangelical thirst for the center

In his exhaustive study of fundamentalism, Martin Marty, suggests that this perspective must feed on what Marty calls "oppositionalism." Most fundamentalists are defined, in part, by what they stand against. It is the fuel of growth. It brings people together, gives them courage, and describes their reliance on one another and on the traditions that have made them unique. The erosion of America's informal state religion provided the fundamentalists with a substantial adversary, and they rallied millions of their fellow citizens committed to stand against this dangerous adversary. The more the courts, and the liberal psyche at their core, officially dismantled the customs which branded the U.S. as a Christian nation, the more evangelicals were determined to defeat this demonic enemy. America would not become an atheistic country. During most of this era, the Soviet Union and the communist philosophy that lay behind it defined America's most serious adversary. And communism was atheistic! Thus the Courts and the liberal set of notions undergirding many of their rulings were patently communistic. Billy James Hargis and Carl McIntire set the agenda. Jerry Falwell and Pat Robertson revised the pattern and used it as a way to solidify the growing power of conservative Christian religion.

Thus the vestige of Christendom may be found in the effort of America's conservative Christians to re-establish a cultural hegemony based on a religion's language, ethic, political alliances, artistic expressions, philosophic constructs, and social contracts. But the flow of history runs against that tide, and the age of Christendom has already come to an end. "The mills of the gods grind slowly, but they grind exceeding fine."

False directions taken by progressives

In Chapter 4 we listed a number of important insights progressives might adopt from their more conservative neighbors. However, scores of progressive churches, seeing the aggressive statistically successful programs of the evangelicals, have taken an unnerving course. Faced with shrinking numbers, declining strength and the loss of a central place in the public square, they have often reverted to a series of defensive measures, which have amounted either to weak responses to the new realities, or efforts to copy their more prosperous evangelical colleagues. They insisted the problem of declining energies could be solved, for instance, by church growth programs. They would gain back their important place, and redress their losses with a series of recruitment strategies. To this end church growth became an operative initiative. During my first years out of seminary I was caught up in this flood of programs. I received hundreds of persons into churches I pastored—as many as 116 in one day. Many of these people I saw on the occasion they joined, but rarely after that. I did not even know many of their names. They had been recruited on the basis that the congregation was a friendly place, made few demands, and expected modest levels of belief, commitment, or sacrifice. A radical Christian faith was watered down to appeal to the least common denominator. "Food, fun, and fellowship for people of all ages and interests," became the central theme.

Progressives also focused on planting new churches. Don McGavaran, a Professor at Fuller Theological Seminary and a former missionary to India, insisted that these new churches focus their attention on what he termed "the homogeneity principle." People, he insisted, are uncomfortable when they have too many borders to cross, thus churches of mixed constituencies are less likely to succeed. Much of the church growth effort, therefore, centered on a variety of ethnically based congregations, or congregations in white middle-class suburbs.

Observing how "successful" evangelical churches tended to use new forms of worship built around a collection of praise songs, scores of progressive churches replaced their hymnbooks with giant projection screens and their hymnals with praise choruses. Praise or "contemporary" worship services were added to their "traditional" liturgical offering.

Across the country many progressive congregations began to downplay their former liberal social action agendas as not conducive to winning new members, principally young families.

While all of these four strategies—church growth, new homogenous congregations, praise services and the soft-pedaling of "peace and justice" were occasionally productive, by and large nothing attempted stemmed the institutional hemorrhaging, and the losses continued. Typical of other mainline denominations, the Christian Church (Disciples of Christ) declined from almost 2 million "participating members" to just over 400,000 in less than four decades.

Images and practices, which had previously defined progressive faith, were virtually abandoned for these softer approaches. Ecumenical commitment gave way to a fixation on congregational solidarity. Solid support of the denomination and interdenominational agencies dramatically waned. Biblical and theological inquiry became transmuted into less demanding internal programs. Ministers saw themselves less as evangelists or theologians and more as Managers or Chief Executive Officers.

None of these modifications, however, managed to penetrate *all* of the previously strong congregations. There were still amazing pockets of vitality. In many places faithfulness replaced success as the hallmark of congregational life. Here and there persisted the realization that as long as a church was fundamentally committed to its own growth, well-being, and sustenance it would be difficult for it to see beyond its own borders. It is only as churches become "decentered" are they open to the moving of the Spirit and to the critical revitalization that must accompany ecclesial reform.

The compelling power of the Commonwealth of God

The progressive church can never hope to attract the attention of the secular world, let along those millions who have been seduced by the political right, unless it has a compelling message which flows from an encounter with Jesus, and demonstrates what he talked about every time he adduced his most powerful and consistent image, "the Commonwealth of God." And when it does, it should not expect to be embraced by a culture whose values and goals are remarkable different.

Only here and there, now and then, among this one and that one will come a salvific encounter with the gospel. Our effort is not to deprogram our seduced brothers and sisters, but to demonstrate the power of Jesus' message. Those who have ears to hear, may hear.

Congregations need again to become centers of thoughtful action rooted in theological inquiry. Congregational ministers need again to see themselves as resident theologians, and not simply managers of small businesses or public relations experts whose main function is to keep the customers happy.

For progressive churches to revert to the successful agenda they had developed in the booming post World War II religious atmosphere will not suffice. We can never go back to the good old days, even if they had once existed.

A post-Christendom view of the Christian message

There is no guarantee that re-visioning the Christian faith and the nature of the church will win back the departed evangelicals, turn the tide for millions of America's seduced Christians, or reposition the progressive church as again being central to our national life. Nevertheless faithfulness demands a rethinking of the nature of congregational life among those in the progressive Christian community. Christendom is gone, and the new post-Christendom wine calls for new wineskins. Consider the following essential restatements as to the nature of lived-out faith:

CHRISTENDOM: A hierarchical system in which authority flows from the top down.

POST-CHRISTENDOM: A system where leadership and direction are shared by those set apart, trained, and commissioned, *and* by those of every rank and status. Domination by clergy must give way to the collective wisdom of all the church.

CHRISTENDOM: A religious structure in which the marginalized are subjects without voice.

POST CHRISTENDOM: New forms of ecclesial life in which the marginalized become mentors for the whole church.

CHRISTENDOM: A propensity for the church to be obsessed with its own growth and institutional health.

POST CHRISTENDOM: A propensity for the church to focus its life on generating evidences of the reign of God.

CHRISTENDOM: Salvation seen as within the church.

POST-CHRISTENDOM: Salvation seen as within the world.

CHRISTENDOM: A church that sees a need to keep itself well positioned within the dominant society.

POST-CHRISTENDOM: A church that is willing to live on the margins of society.

CHRISTENDOM: The use of the Bible as a collection of verses to be employed as tools of truth against outsiders.

POST-CHRISTENDOM: The use of the Bible as a collection of stories, metaphors, celebrations, and testimonies of the grace of God.

CHRISTENDOM: Theology seen as handed-down doctrine—*orthodoxy.*

POST-CHRISTENDOM: Theology seen as doing the truth—*orthopraxis*.

The recovery of courage

Perhaps the greatest current need of the progressive church is to recover its courage so that it is again clear about the meaning of Christian faith. Knowing what it has been called to be, it then moves to embodying ways by which it can live out the implications of that courage. Progressive faith must be clear about the relationship between faithfulness to the gospel and the world beyond ecclesial boundaries. President Ronald Reagan reminded his followers to "stay the course." While many of us might have serious questions about the particular course he counseled his followers to stay, his advice is particularly instructive for the battered progressive movement. To seek solutions to our current difficulties by attempting to mimic our more conservative colleagues, or to abandon the call of Christ to evidence the Commonwealth of God in the world, are both exercises on futility.

Redefining justice

Consider just one aspect of this rediscovered faithfulness. What, for progressive Christians, are the deeper implications of the word "justice"? Following the political definition of the word, many evangelicals tend to believe that justice means punishment. Our evangelical President George W. Bush continually used the word in that light. "We will pursue them and bring them to justice." Justice means capturing, trying, convicting, and sentencing malefactors of all kinds, particularly terrorists. America's justice system is based on police, courts, and prisons.

There is throughout the Biblical record, however, a far different notion of justice. It has been most clearly defined by Walter Brueggemann. Justice is finding out what belongs to whom, and returning it to them. Biblical justice is rooted in human equity. Those who knit farm to farm at the expense of the poor are not just. Justice means that land which has been confiscated by the rich is returned to the poor, so that in God's commonwealth each family can sit under its own vine and fig tree.

Biblical justice implies economic and social inclusion. It demands the shrinking of the increasingly unjust division in which the rich get richer and the poor get poorer. It challenges those economic, political, and social institutions, which regularly favor the haves at the expense of the have-nots.

This sort of Biblical faithfulness may not win back many of the fundamentalists in our midst, but theological authenticity must precede any direct appeal.

CHAPTER 9

The Public Face of Progressive Religion

In the foregoing chapter we talked about the internal stability and faithfulness of the progressive church. We now turn to its public face. As we suggested in the introduction, when people think of the Christian religion these days, they tend to mean a conservative form of evangelicalism, particularly a variety that is attached to right-wing politics. In the public mind Christianity is now identified with conservative religion and its institutions. Nevertheless, the fundamental loss among progressives may not be numerical strength, but courage. We have often denied our own capacity to act boldly. In the next chapter I will list just a few of the possible actions individuals might take in reclaiming the Christian faith from its seducers. In this chapter our focus will be on missional possibilities both for congregations and for their extra-congregational units and agencies. By that we mean their action in society, which we believe must be a major focus in any post-Christendom progressive church.

Reclaiming the Christian faith in congregational life

First we will look at congregations and their programs. As is true of the whole church, the fundamental task of the congregation is to evidence in the world around it, as well as within itself, the nature of the Reign of God. When, therefore, anyone outside the parochial borders observes or is confronted by what the church is and does, they might see demonstrated what Jesus talked about when he described the nature of a society where God's commonwealth is truly present. Clear and courageous answers need to be forthcoming when the secular world beyond the congregation asks crucial questions. It is only as the congregation is able to demonstrate courageous responses to these queries that outsiders will care what has been said.

The world asks, "Who is welcome?"

Consider this question: Who is welcome and who is not? One of the marks of the progressive church—and of what Jesus described as God's commonwealth—is its inclusiveness. Two generations ago "liberal" congregations were known for their racial inclusiveness. When I became pastor of a formerly segregated all-white congregation in Virginia, I knew that the witness of the church in that religious community revolved around its becoming racially inclusive. While the congregation was not officially segregated, that was certainly its unofficial position. Despite the sign on the bulletin board that read, "everyone welcome," we all knew better. In parking lot conversations, the leaders of the church held that although they could not prohibit "Negroes" from attending, they did not need to make them feel particularly welcome. After a number of abortive attempts to induce local "Negroes" to become part of the church, attempts which they rightly viewed with considerable suspicion, I finally imported a family from a nearby African American community, and the church was officially integrated. This action, of course, never solved any long-term racial issue. In fact its artificiality was obvious. Therefore, no one from the African American community rose to the bait. Two fortuitous things did happen, however. The congregation was overwhelming in its welcome of this new family. Even the hardest segregationists found fresh insights, and almost all of them were forced to revise their previous attitudes, especially when the mother in the new family produced a Bible study centered around race and religion. But beyond that, as word spread throughout the community, a number of people who had long since given up on finding an affirming liberal church took notice. The black family and two of the older white church members were interviewed by the local newspaper, and word of the action spread. Nobody believed that such a thing could happen in Virginia. Even a few previously hard-core conservatives were persuaded that what was going on had the earmarks of Biblical authenticity. A few right-leaning former members were lured back to the church as conversations spread around the community.

Although the church in our day has not solved or in many places even seriously addressed the question of race, that is not the only issue which currently gets our attention.

Today's "inclusive" issue is likely to be focused on homosexuality.

What happened when another congregation with which I had been acquainted began to look seriously at that question? After a long and sometimes heated Bible study, the congregation voted to become "open and affirming." At that point most members were unaware that already a handful of closeted gay and lesbian persons had long since become members. Slowly they became open about their orientation. The changes, both internally and in the community, were dramatic. The large outdoor signboard now read, "This congregation is open and affirming"—clear code words. Very few weeks went by when there was not some celebration of the fact in public worship, and there was generated a visible support group in the congregation. A newspaper wrote a feature story about the church, and other homosexual people who had been driven out of their former congregations found a new church home. In addition, a few straight people who wanted to be part of a church that was willing to take an "open and affirming" stand rallied in support. Even a handful of formerly right-wingers were able to celebrate the bold, forthright, newly discovered mission of that congregation. While this public action by the congregation also hardened opposition and rejection in some other evangelical circles, a significant number of former secularists and even political conservatives were encouraged to join in a discussion of the gay issue—more properly called, the homophobic issue.

In both of the cases I have cited, it was the courageous action of the congregation *and* the public presentation of that action that mattered. I know of other churches that, if asked whether they are open to gay and lesbian persons, would say, "Yes. We even have our open position in a printed document you can find in the pew racks." But most church members are unaware of the policy. Nothing is said about it in worship or other aspects of church life. There is no Biblical basis the congregation has studied, and certainly nobody in the community has the slightest idea that the church has taken that stand. No un-closeted gay or lesbian persons have surfaced either in the membership or from the community.

The question as to who is welcome and who is not is a profoundly Biblical matter. Even in congregations that know the importance of this issue, there is often a hesitancy to do as much as discussing it. I have heard pastors say," We have already sustained more losses than we can comfortably afford, and to raise that issue might set us back even farther." It is this failure of courage, which will never position even a progressive congregation to be affirmed or even noticed.

The world asks, "what about justice?"

There are many other ways in which congregations can witness before the community to their clarity about the implications of the gospel. Most churches, including many on the religious right, are deeply committed to ministries of compassion. In hundreds of communities it is the more conservative congregations that spend considerable amounts of money on food kitchens, homeless shelters, drug and alcohol recovery programs, and homes for pregnant young women. We should celebrate this witness. But progressive congregations, who have studied their way to clarity about the implications of the gospel, can move publicly beyond charity to justice. In doing so they may well get the attention of their communities—although that is a by-product, not the basic reason for the activity.

In one very conservative community a number of more progressive churches began a noontime program to feed the hungry. All one had to do was show up at the Open Door Food Kitchen from 11 to 1 every day of the year to receive a nourishing meal. Most of the right-leaning churches in town first agreed to participate in this venture, but later withdrew when it became obvious the goal was nutrition, not evangelism. There were no sermons, altar calls or even tracts inviting the hungry to one or another of the congregations. From two hundred to four hundred people were fed every day. The participating churches were justly proud of what they had done. After more than five years of these daily meals, a few members of the sponsoring congregations began to raise the justice question. Why, in that prosperous middle-class community, were there that many hungry people? Wasn't adequate nutrition a human right? State legislatives and national officials were brought into the conversations. The discussions were well covered in the local press. Here were churches that were not only dedicated to ministries of compassion, but were also now involved in the deeper questions of justice. Sensitive members of more right-wing congregations were also caught up in the discussion, and the issue became a bridge between the two bodies of Christians.

The world asks, "What about values?"

Can congregations involve themselves in what is or appears to be political action where the question of values becomes concrete? Conservative churches in our era seem to have no problem with overt partisan activities. In recent elections, hundreds of thousands of pamphlets were put on windshields in church parking lots. Many conservative ministers made direct appeals to their congregations to support this candidate and reject that candidate.

Progressive congregations are much more hesitant to be directly involved at that level. Nevertheless, much of the political dialogue these days focuses on values which have direct political implications. The values question has been widely used by the Christian right. The popular press describes the culture wars as being fought out between those who hold religious values and those who do not. But these values have been limited to the three issues defined as such by the religious right: abortion, homosexuality and a "Christian identity" in public places and in public policy.

Progressive churches must redefine the nature of substantial Christian values. Among them are: preemptive war, the unilateral right to massively interfere in the domestic policies and governments of any other nation we choose to reorder, world domination, the military control of space, the sole right to have and use weapons of mass destruction, torture, civil liberties, tax policies, the shredding of the social safety net, the degradation of God's nature for the sake of profits, the hostility of much of the world's people, trillions of dollars of debt future generations will be forced to pay, the proliferation of guns in the hands of practically everybody, the death penalty—just to name a few.

These values questions came in the package with abortion, homosexuality, and Christian identity in public places. Conservative Christians were seduced into buying the whole package without seriously evaluating its content. Many devout conservative Christians do not accept many of the items in the package. Here lies a possibility for progressive congregations to act publicly, in the name of Christian values, in each of the above listed areas. This can be done without once mentioning candidates or political parties, and yet the political implications are enormous. If there is to be public discussion of the values question, progressive churches must set the terms of the agenda. Too often we have argued on the grounds set by the evangelical right.

When there are public demonstrations around any of these issues, congregations ought to participate using signs, banners, and handouts carrying the name of the church. Pro-action must replace re-action. Many conservative Christians have never heard a serious discussion of most of these concerns, and the thoughtful among them might well reshape their opinions or at least understand that there is Christian, Biblically based room for discussion. As long as we allow the values issue to focus only on abortion and gay marriage, we have missed not only important opportunities, but also a serious confrontation with the ethical demands of the Christian faith.

The role of the church beyond congregations

There is considerable evidence these days that denominations and denominationalism have begun to approach their use-by dates. Few seriously hold that the best days for the various bodies, formerly called mainline churches, are ahead of them. While there may be sufficient reasons to take these predictions seriously, the announced death of these bodies may be premature. Their hope may not be in getting larger, but in getting smaller and becoming dedicated activists.

A case in point. Each year for the past three decades, The United Church of Christ has seen a decline in its membership. By 2004 it was faced with a serious decision. Either it could huddle quietly in the middle of the road, attempting to appeal to groups on the right and on the left of church life, or it could summon the courage to confront the religious and political right wing, not by attacking these strongholds of American piety, but by being clear publicly about its own understanding of the gospel. It chose the latter course. In that year it developed a widely seen brace of television ads, which focused on its inclusive policies. These ads showed, among other things, gay couples being received in the church when others had turned them away. The theme focused on God's extravagant welcome—and the church's. The networks turned down the ads as being controversial. After all, President Bush had taken a very different religious stance. Cable networks and stations, including Fox News, did run the ads, and the UCC website recorded tens of thousands of hits. People across the country responded, and in the weeks that followed significant numbers of newcomers showed up at a variety of UCC congregations. While many of these people happened to be gay and lesbian, there were also a variety of others. This new group included former members of more conservative church bodies, who had become disillusioned with their former narrow groups, and even a few hard-core conservatives who sensed the authenticity of the church's message.

At the July 2005 meeting of the General Synod of the United Church of Christ, a resolution was passed supporting same-sex marriage. The day the action was taken, it was covered on the evening news by most networks including the "NewsHour with Jim Lehrer." Major stories ran the next day in most of America's major papers. Here was the Christian faith presented in other than the usual evangelical right-wing format. The Church did not take the position it did in order to get public attention, but the attention was a positive added value. At least a significant portion of the American people were confronted by a solid Christian witness which was not tied to the political right.

While these actions also resulted in losses of a scattering of members and congregations, the issue was faithfulness to the gospel and not numerical growth. Other denominations have taken a different approach, and are sitting quietly in the middle of the road, or are attempting to emulate the successful appearing tactics of churches in the religious right. This cautious approach has not stemmed the hemorrhaging, as they slowly await denominational death—or at least spiritual senility.

Councils of Churches, local, national and worldwide, have also faced a similar erosion of numerical strength. Since they tend to be mainly composed of mainline denominations, their decline has followed that of their constituencies.

Like some of their member units, the National Council of Churches has not chosen the safer path. One example: In June 2005 the Council released a statement on the war against Iraq. Included in the statement were five NO propositions and five YES propositions.

Some excerpts:

> NO to leaders who have sent many honorable sons and daughters to fight a dishonorable war.
> NO to the violence that has cost 1700 American lives (the number now exceeds 4,000)…and killed untold numbers of Iraqis.
> NO to the abuse of prisoners that has shamed our nation.
> NO to the price tag for this war, which has rendered our federal budget incapable of adequately caring for the poorest of our own citizens.
> NO to theologies that demonize other nations and religions.
> YES to foreign policies that seek justice rather than domination.
> YES to an early fixed timetable for the withdrawal of United States troops.
> YES to human rights even for our enemies.

YES to spending and taxing priorities that poor the poor first.

YES to a restoration of truth telling in the public square and "last resort" rather than "first strike" as a criterion for the use of force to restrain evil.

During the July 4th weekend this statement was printed in newspapers all across the nation and signed by tens of thousands of American citizens. In Claremont, California, for instance, the signatures and the statement occupied a three-page, multicolored spread.

If the general population had believed that the Christian faith was limited to the religious right, these examples from congregations to the National Council of Churches ought to have modified, if not dismantled that prejudice.

Did these activities win back from the political right many sincere Christians? Perhaps not many, but at least some. And at least a few million Americans believed they had to take a hard look at the ethical and value issues that had formerly been in the sole possession of evangelicals.

CHAPTER 10

Taking Back the Christian Faith—By One of Us at a Time

While we must rely on traditional progressive institutions to reclaim the Christian faith from those who have captured it, we turn finally to a few of the ways in which individual progressive Christians can take action.

Finding Emerging Para-church Organizations

Across the nation there is a growing network of newly organized movements that have taken the Christian imperative seriously, but are not held within the institutional boundaries of traditional congregations and their denominations. They can do what structured church bodies may not be able to do. Most congregations are composed of a broad spectrum of persons, whose diverse opinions on significant social issues inhibit action. Many of the emerging para-church bodies may not be so constrained.

The proliferation of these units is so rapid that it would be impossible to offer a current list. But one only needs to find them in almost every significant community working alongside progressive congregations. Let me cite just one current example.

In the last decade of the 20th century, two prominent theologians and church leaders, John Cobb and George Regis, developed in the Los Angeles area a theological think-tank, which produced a series of thoughtful papers, and finally a small collection of books analyzing significant issues confronting society. Early in this century The Project for the Human Family was transformed into a much more active institution under the name Progressive Christians Uniting. The resultant body sought to bring together Christians from across the Los Angeles area, who were dedicated to direct action in a broad variety of "liberal" causes. Among them: the war against Iraq and American foreign policy in general, civil liberties, civil rights for Gay and Lesbian persons—particularly in regard to marriage laws—prison reform, gender equality, global warming and other significant ecological issues, just immigration guidelines, and a host of issues confronting local communities. Since its inception, PCU has spawned a number of local chapters throughout the Los Angeles area, and beyond.

Participation in the work of PCU—there is really no formal membership—comes from four sources: 1-congregations and their denominations dedicated to progressive Christian concerns

2-progressive members of more conservative or ideologically mixed congregations 3-Persons who have long since left traditional congregations and who have been looking for an alternative. 4-People of dedicated good will who might never have been part of any formal religious body, but whose ethic and commitments are in harmony with those who have.

With the increased visibility of this organization, hundreds of progressive Christians have found colleagues committed to action for the common good. Individual Christians looking for ways to engage societal issues without the constraint often found in traditional congregations and their assorted ecclesial bodies, may find a similar para-church structure nearby.

It should be noted that in most communities there are also inter-faith bodies, which include progressives from Muslim, Jewish, and other religious bodies that do similar solid work. Those like PCU which carry the name "Christian" do so as a public testimony that not all Christians are captives of the religious/political right wing. If most people are convinced that "Christian" means only adherents of the Falwell, Robertson, and Dobson brands of religious and political conviction, these para-church bodies offer a clear public alternative. Individuals looking for ways to witness to progressive religious faith, which might help take the gospel back from the political right wing, may find it in one of these generative bodies.

Discovering Non-Religious Colleagues

We can never assume that progressive religion and progressive religious institutions have all the answers to the production of positive social change.

There are in our communities significant numbers of secular organizations with whom we share common commitments. Consider: the ACLU, MoveOn, progressive newspapers, YouTube, blogs and other freshly minted internet resources, local and national political parties, Colleges and Universities, Social Service organizations, Planned parenthood and other bodies that support "Choice," organizations of Gays and Lesbians, a variety of peace networks, individuals not part of any organization with whom we share progressive perspectives—the list goes on an on. Find them in your community and make common cause in supporting the issues important to many of us in the progressive religious world.

Biblical and Theological Clarity

As Christians we have a solid theological base for how we view the world. The Christian ethic is substantially based on the ethic expounded by Jesus in his continual emphasis on the Commonwealth of God. We do not view the world only through secular eyes. We have in the whole Christian tradition a worldview that may be substantially different than that which society is currently espousing. It is our obligation to know what it is and to relate it to what we find in the world around us.

The Bible is our sourcebook for a progressive social ethic, not in the use of proof texts or other Biblical snippets, but in the great broad themes of justice, peace, and inclusion which stand at the heart of the Judeo-Christian tradition.

Witnessing from the Inside

A few hardy progressive souls may assist in taking back the Christian faith from the inside of basically conservative religious institutions. Consider the following scenario.

Sally E. has been a member of a progressive congregation. There is in her community a large evangelical congregation which dominates the Christian witness in that city. It regularly proclaims its support of the war against Iraq, condemns homosexuality, believes all abortion should be outlawed, supports capital punishment, stands against any effort to control the proliferation of firearms and believes God has ordained the United States as hope of the world.

This congregation, however, has a solid record of supporting the needy in its community through a food and clothing program and a shelter for the homeless.

Sally knows some members of this church and begins to attend its services. In addition, she volunteers each week at their food bank. She finds those with whom she shares this activity to be dedicated, highly motivated people. Over a period of time Sally discovers occasions to talk with her newfound friends about perspectives on some of the issues these good people had not considered. She is not argumentative or abrasive, and stays within the teachings of Jesus as her model. She listens before she talks. She is able to articulate the position of her conservative friends so well that they can say, "Yes, that's what we believe." This buys her the right to state points of view not otherwise found in that congregation. And she is heard, if not readily agreed with.

Is this sort of infiltration effective? In one sense, it is subversive, but in another sense, the only way to understand what someone with an opposing point of view really believes is to see their point of view from the inside. Simultaneously, personal contact instead of ideological debate is far more effective in producing new ways to thinking, or at least in the initiation of a responsible dialogue. In some cases persons like Sally may even join conservative churches as a way to bring influence from the inside.

Direct Political Activity

Churches, and other overtly religious institutions, must exercise a responsible observance of the boundary between church and state. Nevertheless, individual Christians must realize that "politics" is not a dirty word, and there are occasions when people of faith need to be profoundly involved in public affairs, political parties, legislative matters and elections. Responsible faith demands solid attention to public policy.

It may start with informed letter writing, not only to public officials, but also to the editors of newspapers and other avenues of opinion. The proliferation of the internet offers amazing possibilities to stay informed about the serious issues facing the body politic. Good, thoughtful writers might consider initiating or participating in a political or public affairs blog.

I am personally deeply involved in a local party as well as serving on the Board of Directors of a think tank, "The American Institute for Progressive Democracy." Look around your community and you will find places where you can be creatively involved.

Voter registration drives, phone banks and other organizational work for progressive candidates, and serious conversations with friends, neighbors, business associates, and even golf partners may be part of the generative mix.

The agenda found in the following addendum may provide clues as to the progressive content of public affairs. It is no longer good enough to sit back and loudly moan about "them," or to be reduced to "aren't they terrible" or "ain't it a shame."

Creative Christians cannot simply rely on others or somebody else's organization to make the witness. If not you, then who? While it is true that Christians are usually made twelve at a time, that does not obviate the power or importance of what one progressive person can do.

I conclude this book with an addition, spelling out what might be the content of a vital public agenda for the reclaimed Christian church. This addendum spells out 1-what we essentially believe about the common life of our people, 2-the middle principles which would move us in that direction, 3-and a few of the specific proposals which progressive Christians might support.

ADDENDUM

A Progressive Manifesto for Christians in the United States

THE PROLOGUE

Progressive Christians believe that there is inherent in the Judeo/Christian tradition clear points of view about the society in which the gospel becomes incarnated. This manifesto is divided into three sections. Section I -The Credo. This We Believe. Section II -A Vision which flows from these basic social convictions. Section III - Implementing the Vision through Specific Programs. This Manifesto is not a theological statement using traditional religious language. It is rather a statement in secular terms of what we believe flows from our faith as revealed in the Biblical witness, particularly in the life and teachings of Jesus as he identified the nature of the coming Commonwealth of God, and how this applies to issues facing American society.

SECTION I
The Credo

THIS WE BELIEVE

WE BELIEVE that the health of any people derives from the relationship between individuals and the society in which they live. We were created to be in community with others.

WE BELIEVE that all human beings have within them the potential for both good and evil, and that social structures, beginning with the family, and including the institutions of the larger society, potentially foster the best about both individual and cultural existence.

WE BELIEVE that Progressive Christians are called to both create and support those cooperative structures, which foster the potential for goodness in a commonwealth of mutual support.

WE BELIEVE that human beings are more than solitary individuals, and reject the notion that persons must live selfish lives, seeking only their own wealth, comfort, and self-advancement.

WE BELIEVE that individuals thrive when they are supported by life-giving social institutions beginning with strong families, community-based schools, progressive religious structures, and responsible public services. We hold that members of a civil society must work together to provide those institutions.

WE BELIEVE that while nations should seek their own paths in defense of their own national goals, structures such as the United Nations are essential in working toward the goal of making military force a monopoly of the international community.

WE BELIEVE that military power should be employed by individual nations only for self-defense, and that the Christian gospel suggests other reconciling ways to resolve conflict among persons and nations.

WE BELIEVE that these are the fundamental values which must animate the vision of a fair and just commonwealth of mutual respect, and thus form the basis for the programs and projects of progressive people of all sorts and convictions.

WE BELIEVE that these basic values are not only in harmony with the message of Jesus, but also flow from his image of the commonwealth of God which he proclaimed.

SECTION II
The Vision

AMERICA'S ROLE IN THE WORLD

Our vision of the role of America in today's world grows out of the core values articulated in the CREDO. Before we can design a roadmap, we must have a clear direction. Thus we offer this vision of what a progressive understanding of Christian faith might look like when translated into national values and goals. If our nation is to pull back from the brink, we must deepen our understanding of where we ought to go, and summon an extraordinary will in calling the nation to it without compromising the essential wall of separation between church and state.

Our goals must be no less than to heal the world by casting a vision leading to specific plans and programs for the generation of a better future in which people will learn to live in harmony and goodwill, both at home and abroad.

While we reject the notion that the state and its laws should be based on the teaching of any particular religious creed, we believe that the spirit of all great world religions leads to a more whole world, and further that these goals are in harmony with progressive Christian affirmations.

The Preservation of this Fragile Planet

WE ENVISION a world society focused on the care and preservation of this God-given planet—our common home. The immediate threat of global warming must be a primary concern; a threat which must be brought under control beginning immediately. It must be a primary concern at every level of national life, so that this disaster does not overtake mankind, and so that the quest for economic development does not permit our universal human home to be despoiled. Progressive Christians should deliver a clarion call to make a livable world its top priority. To do less is to turn our backs on reality and to betray our descendents and our religious commitments.

America's Place the Family of Nations

WE ENVISION America, currently the world's richest most powerful nation, increasingly involved in working to share in the development of paths for peace and equity among the world's people. While coming to grips with our overwhelming power, we do not see America as seeking to dominate or exploit others, nor do we intend to dictate to others the forms of government under which they are to live.

WE ENVISION a world as a family of peoples, each nation pursuing its own path to fulfillment through the development of social, political and religious structures of freedom and equality, which make for a decent, secure life for all their people.

The United Nations

WE ENVISION a world community in which the United Nations has our support as the world's primary peacekeeping authority.

A Nuclear Weapon-free World

WE ENVISION a nuclear-free world in which all atomic and thermo-nuclear weaponry have been abolished. The existence of nuclear weapons may eventually doom the species, as some madman or rogue nation may instigate a nuclear holocaust.

A Fair Distribution of the World's Wealth

WE ENVISION a world where poverty among the world's people is substantially reduced, as ways are found to share the planet's abundant resources. While preserving a decent and dignified way of life for our posterity, we commit ourselves to assist others to live under such conditions. In the process we may discover that the unlimited consumption of resources may not be the assured way to human happiness and fulfillment. We acknowledge that the people of the United States consume a disproportionate share of these resources, and that a world divided between the very rich and the very poor is an unjust and unstable world. We envision a more just world which bears the marks of what Jesus described as the commonwealth or reign of God.

AMERICA'S DOMESTIC VISION

The goals of our commonwealth will only be realized as our people join to work together for the common good. We progressive Christians articulate the following domestic vision as a call for a society where every person is treated with respect and dignity.

Civil Rights and Civil Liberties

WE ENVISION the full and fair restoration of the provisions of the Bill of Rights and the strict limitation of both legislation and judicial decisions that compromise civil liberties. We repudiate the notion that any current national emergency or the overarching needs of security justify compromising the "Bill of Rights" or infringing on civil liberties. As substantial to that infringement we include emergency legislation instituted since September 11, 2001.

The Fair Distribution of Domestic Resources

WE ENVISION a democracy without sharp divisions between the very rich and the very poor, through tax policies designed to assure that all citizens contribute a proportionate share to the general welfare.

Health Care

WE ENVISION a universal health care system delivered at minimum administrative cost and available to every man, woman, and child of this land. While the road may be arduous, and although segments of society will be justifiably fearful of losing their place—insurance companies, HMOs, health providers, for instance—the goal is clear. At the same time we recognize the difficulties that lie in the path of achieving that goal. We hold that it is incumbent on the commonwealth to care for all its citizens, particularly the most fragile and vulnerable.

Gender Equality

WE ENVISION the extension of equal rights to all women in American society. We affirm the principle of choice in the area of reproductive rights, and we are committed to the social support of all children, both by families and by the larger community. While great strides have recently been made securing the basic rights of half of our population who are women, much remains to be done to end their unequal status.

Migration

WE ENVISION the generation of a responsible and just policy to welcome and control immigration to the United States. We recognize that while migrations often create hardships, they also generate opportunities both for the migrants and the people already inhabiting the land. We realize that the present irrational policies of our government often create unacceptable hardships for the people who come here hoping to find a better life.

WE ENVISION the dismantling of arbitrary rules set by national governments, tribal groups or religious fanatics. We look for a time when those on the move from place to place will be relieved of the suffering and distress they often encounter, and we look for a rational system which protects the rights of those already residing in a particular area, and the hopes of those seeking a new way of life in a new place. At the same time, we recognize the hardships forced upon workers already in this country, whose livelihood is threatened by the influx of cheap labor.

SECTION III
Implementing the Vision

THROUGH SPECIFIC POLICIES

The specific proposals that follow flow both from our initial affirmations and the vision we have articulated in the previous section. They are not intended to be an exhaustive list or to serve only as a political agenda. They are, however, clearly defined social goals available to our commonwealth in both its public and private spheres of power.

OUR ROLE IN THE WORLD

Progressive Christians view the role of the United States as that of one country in a family of nations, willing and determined to contribute to the welfare of the world community in ways commensurate with our ideals and strengths. We are determined to use our great resources to alleviate poverty, misery, and disease around the world.

The Preservation of this Fragile Planet

The most critical issue before the world may well be the preservation of this fragile planet. It is the only home any of us have. Al Gore in his *An Inconvenient Truth* demonstrates how our heedless economic expansion and our addiction to oil poses a mortal danger to our natural habitat. Global warming threatens to upset the balance of nature on which our lives depend.

WE THEREFORE PROPOSE the immediate ratification of the Kyoto Treaty, or its subsequent revisions, to reduce greenhouse gas emissions. We further propose that we make major investments in alternative fuel research, and generate support for public transit. While these proposals also relate to domestic policies, more than any other arena they have worldwide implications.

America's Place in the Family of Nations

WE PROPOSE that Progressive Christians repudiate any political doctrine which calls the United States to world domination, such as the Security Documents of September 2002 and March 2006. In addition, we propose Progressive Christians call for a NO FIRST NUCLEAR STRIKE pledge, and a repudiation of the doctrine of PREEMPTIVE WAR. We further propose the rejection of the notion of American empire, and call for the dismantling of American military bases not strictly necessary for our security.

WE PROPOSE that the United States immediately refrain from the use of military force to insure our will or force the installation of regimes that are patterned after our own democratic institutions. In particular, we are committed to refrain from any unilateral preemptive military attack on another sovereign nation. We will end the tragic occupation of Iraq, find the appropriate mechanism to bring our troops home, and build structures of peaceful co-existence both in the Near East and in other troubled places of the world.

The United Nations

WE PROPOSE that progressive Christians call the United States to participate in the work of the United Nations without reservation.

Progressive Christians challenge the nation's leadership to fully support the level of the Millennium Project, which is our fair share—namely .7% of the GNP.

A Nuclear Free World

WE PROPOSE that the United States take the leadership in a program whose ultimate goal is the total abolition of all nuclear armaments. We propose the re-affirmation of the non-proliferation program, rejecting any further exceptions.

WE PROPOSE the discontinuation of the present policy designed to put weapons in space.

Toward a Fair Distribution of the World's Wealth

WE PROPOSE that America exercise its gifts and its unrivaled power by the increased use of its resources to significantly alleviate world poverty, as we dedicate a responsible percentage of our national wealth to the healing of the nations, matching the proportional generosity of other developed nations

WE PROPOSE a reconsideration of treaties, which tend to make the rich of the world richer and the poor poorer.

WE PROPOSE a redefinition of the work of the World Bank and the International Monetary Fund so that they may provide assistance to the poorer nations of the world without saddling them with the unpayable debts, which continue to gut their own economies.

OTHER INTERNATIONAL ISSUES
American Policies and the Middle East

The United States must take the lead in resolving the problems of the Middle East. The first clear step is the constructive resolution of the conflict regarding Palestine. No larger resolution of these complex issues will result without a resolution of the Palestinian question.

WE PROPOSE the immediate return of the United States as a fully involved neutral mediator. We believe that negotiations must lead to a secure Israeli state essentially within its pre-1976 boundaries, with Jerusalem as the capital of both the Israeli state and a Palestinian state, with a contiguous and viable Palestinian state on the West Bank, with a secure connection to Gaza. We propose the return to a peaceful solution along the lines of the Geneva Accord of 2003.

REVISITING AMERICA'S DOMESTIC AGENDA

If America is to realize the goals inherent in our commonwealth, it is vital that the people work together as those who share a common vision. Therefore, progressive Christians propose the following:

Civil Rights and Civil Liberties

WE PROPOSE the restoration of the full range of Civil Rights and Liberties bestowed by the Founding Fathers in the Bill of Rights; liberties which have been eroded in the name of security.

The Fair Distribution of Domestic Resources

In recent years there has been an alarming increase in the disparity between rich and poor in America.

WE PROPOSE specific programs in support of raising minimum wage rates.

WE PROPOSE the improvement of services delivered to the general population--such as housing, health care, and public education as well as improved grant and loan programs for qualified students wishing to attend institutions of higher education.

Health Care

WE PROPOSE a commitment to a system of universal health care. Every person in this commonwealth is entitled to adequate medical insurance. We propose the establishment of a single payer system, following the close examination of workable systems in other developed nations.

WE PROPOSE the establishment of a carefully planned system for the retraining and reemployment of persons whose current jobs would be eliminated under a new universal system.

WE PROPOSE a national program, in conjunction with the medical community, to train the additional medical personnel needed to staff a universal system.

WE PROPOSE a plan whereby the additional costs of a universal system be met in part through the enormous savings resulting from the implementation of such a system. We also seek the experience of other developed nations, whose percentage of their GNP dedicated to health care is far less than ours, while the level of care shown in terms of infant mortality, life expectance and other indices, often far exceeds that of the United States.

WE PROPOSE an honest evaluation of the impact of the possible limitation and rationing of resources, especially costly procedures among our most elderly citizens. We further propose that we seek the counsel of religious leaders and other ethicists in considering the implications of medical care in which resources need to be shared rationally and compassionately.

Gender equality

WE PROPOSE legislation which secures the safety of those supporting the right of choice for women regarding their reproductive health and freedom.

WE PROPOSE the full implementation of both legislation and administrative directives calling for equal pay for equal work.

WE PROPOSE legislation which will protect the full civil rights of Gay, Lesbian, bi-sexual and transgender persons, particularly in regard to marriage laws in the various States.

Other Issues and Concerns

While we have reviewed several of the critical problems facing the United States and on which progressive Christians must take clear positions, there are many other matters that fall within the orbit of our concern. We include, for example, explicit action leading to the following:

The reformation of the penal system, including the repudiation of the three strikes law, the inequity involved in issues surrounding probation, capital punishment and prison management.

The decriminalization of certain recreational drugs.

The development of renewable energy resources, with the concomitant loss of dependence on non-renewable resources.

The support and adequate funding of public education.

The critical support of organized labor.

The control of the proliferation of firearms and a reinterpretation of the Second Amendment of the U.S. Constitution.

Conclusion

We return to the Basic Principles stated in our CREDO. We yearn for the Good Life for ourselves and our children, and for all the people of this nation, who live in a Commonwealth that nourishes and protects every person. While fully conscious of the dangers inherent in the current world scene, we proudly urge our fellow citizens to seize the opportunities that lie before us to create a more just and peaceful world that enables all the world's children to live secure and satisfying lives

Printed in the United States
203963BV00004B/166-246/P